THE PARISH AS
COVENANT

A CALL TO PASTORAL PARTNERSHIP

THE PARISH AS COVENANT

A CALL TO PASTORAL PARTNERSHIP

THOMAS P. SWEETSER, S.J.

FOREWORD BY **BISHOP KENNETH UNTENER**

SHEED & WARD

Lanham, Chicago, New York, Oxford

As an apostolate of the Priests of the Sacred Heart, a Catholic religious congregation, the mission of Sheed & Ward is to publish books of contemporary impact and enduring merit in Catholic Christian thought and action. The books published, however, reflect the opinion of their authors and are not meant to represent the official position of the Priests of the Sacred Heart.

Published by Sheed & Ward
An Imprint of the Rowman & Littlefield
Publishers, Inc.
4720 Boston Way
Lanham, MD 20706
PO Box 317
Oxford
OX2 9RU, UK

Copyright © 2001 by Thomas P. Sweetser, S.J.

Printed in the United States of America

Cover and interior design: Robin Costa Booth
Cover art commissioned and used with permission from Robin Costa Booth
Scripture quotations are from the New Revised Standard Version of the Bible.

Library of Congress Cataloging-in-Publication Data

Sweetser, Thomas P.
 The parish as covenant : a call to pastoral partnership / Thomas P. Sweetser.
  p. cm.
 Includes bibliographical references and index.
 ISBN 1-58051-110-4
 1. Pastoral theology—Catholic Church. 2. Group ministry—Catholic Church.
 I. Title.
BX1913.S936.2001
253—dc21   2001040088

DEDICATION

In memory of my father,
Dr. Theodore H. Sweetser, Sr.,
whose creative mind and
common sense has been
an inspiration to me
from my earliest days.

CONTENTS

ACKNOWLEDGMENTS

There are many people to thank for their contributions in bringing this volume to completion. Top on the list is my sister, Kathleen M. Hage who changed a rough draft into a readable manuscript. My partners at the Parish Evaluation Project, Sr. Peg Bishop, OSF, and Debora A. Ebratt, not only helped with the editing, they added their own insights and wisdom to the work and put up with my many writing moods over the months.

My thanks to Bishop Kenneth E. Untener, STD. DD., for writing the foreword, and to Frs. Robert J. Kinkel and John L. Doyle, Sr. Virginia Scally, SNDdeN, Gerald P. Roth, and Patrick J. Russell for adding their creative insights regarding pastoral leadership and parish life.

Others have helped with suggestions and valuable editing, including Sr. Mary Benet McKinney, OSB, Fr. Richard P. Abert, SJ, Stephanie J. Russell, Maureen Kelly, and Thomas P. New. A debt of gratitude also goes to Jeremy Langford of Sheed & Ward for agreeing to publish this book and for being patient with missed deadlines.

A debt of gratitude goes to friends and family members who helped with the financial costs involved in the preparation of the manuscript. These include The Sweetser Family Foundation, Jerry and Mary Ann Pearson, Jack and Maureen Kelly, Sally and Jack Daniels, Carol and Bill Moran, Anne and Bob McArthur, Margaret and Ed Hagerty, and Diane Tate and Jackie Brinchley.

Finally, I would like to thank the many leaders and people from parishes across the country who have invited us into their midst and have allowed us to share their ups and downs, the glories and the pitfalls, the successes and the "still working on it" aspects of parish life and operation. The People of God, in dazzling shapes and colors, are the Church.

FOREWORD

By

Bishop Kenneth E. Untener, STD., DD.

There was a time when, at least so it seemed, the parish belonged to the pastor. He could treat it as his own, and the church building, the school, the programs took shape according to his image.

Much of that is changing. We might be tempted to say, "The parish belongs to the parishioners." But a parish is no more the possession of the parishioners than the pastor. The parish belongs to the Church, the whole Church. It is an attempt to become, in a specific place, the Body of Christ.

What this means is that a parish can never simply be the highly motivated religious self-expression of one community. It differs from a house that a family builds according to its tastes or a club that members shape to be what they want for themselves and their families.

Those charged with shaping a parish should be aware of the subtle temptation we are warned against in the First Commandment—the temptation to shape God in our image.

Father Tom Sweetser has set forth some practical ways in which parishes can live up to their call to become more fully the Body of Christ. These suggestions are born of experience. But we learn such things "in the doing," and it will take a lot of "doing" to see how well they work. The Church is at its best when its rituals and structures draw from the wisdom learned in practice, not in theory.

One of the reasons why the Church in the United States is so strong is that its strength lies in *parishes*. In some places in the world today, the emphasis is more on "movements." These attract people who are drawn to the particular charism embodied by the movement, much as candidates are drawn to a particular religious community. Parishes, however, include a wide range of people whose bonds go much deeper — to the roots of our faith. Because of this, they include widely diverse people.

In that sense, forming a parish is much more difficult than forming a movement. The 21,000 plus parishes in the United States, on the whole, have managed to do this well over the long haul. This book will contribute to our ongoing efforts.

Ken Untener
Bishop of Saginaw, Michigan

INTRODUCTION:
How This Came About

*I will make with them a covenant of peace; it shall be
an everlasting covenant with them, and I will multiply them,
and put my sanctuary among them forever.*
— EZEKIEL 37:27

The Church is here to stay. That is the promise. Each week in countless parishes across the country people gather to give thanks, celebrate Eucharist, share faith, support one another, learn Gospel values and gain strength to be servants in their everyday lives. As my own experience working with parishes and as Paul Wilkes' *Excellent Catholic Parishes* give witness to, there is much to be praised about present-day parish life: Children are learning about their faith through family formation and lectionary-based catechesis. Teenagers are becoming enthusiastic about liturgy and communal prayer through Life Teen experiences, which was first introduced by Fr. Dale Fushek of St. Timothy's in Mesa, Arizona, and is now used in various forms in many parishes throughout the country. Young adults are becoming active members in parishes where special efforts are made to invite their involvement and to pay attention to their unique needs and aspirations. Inactive Catholics are finding a home in parishes that cry out, "All Are Welcome," "There Is Room For Everyone," "Come, Be At Home With Us." Divorced and separated, gay and lesbian, handicapped and disadvantaged, elderly and homebound, the disaffected, the poor and the lonely — all are having their needs addressed. They are finding a voice and a rightful place in the Catholic assembly. All this is to be praised. And those who are responsible for these initiatives are to be acknowledged for their efforts.

This, however, is not the whole story. Many Catholic parishes are caught in a Church system that is not working. Priests are being spread too thin and are becoming exhausted and frustrated. Pastoral staffs, even in parishes that are successful in their operation, are growing impatient with a Church structure that asks for their allegiance and obedience while, at the same time, not providing them with a chance to participate in its decision making. Parish leaders look at the untapped potential of the parishioners and wonder how to bring life to the parish. Many who attend Mass leave church uninspired and undernourished. The number who have quit attending church altogether is growing, and as they drift further and further away from the Church, they are taking their children with them.

As mentioned earlier, there are exceptions and positive examples, but the typical Catholic parish stands in need of revitalization and renewed energy. The overarching problem is that the present way the parish is structured depends too heavily on one pastor and puts limits on its effectiveness. (When referring to "pastor" I am speaking of both men and women. Many Catholic parishes are given direction and leadership by someone who is not ordained but functions as the resident pastor. While the name for this position varies with each diocese, the most common terms now being used are "pastoral administrator" or "parish director." A sacramental minister — that is, an ordained priest — comes into the parish to preside at Eucharist and administer sacraments.) If the pastor is vibrant, confident in his or her abilities, not threatened by other people's skills and insights, empowering, and able to share the decision making, then the parish has a bright future. But what if the pastor moves to another community or role in Church life? Or if the pastor is unwilling to share responsibilities, is limited in vision, and/or is facing burnout?

The thesis of this book is that in order to assure a more productive and successful future for the Catholic parish, a change of system is necessary. At the present moment, too much depends upon the creativity, initiative, and leadership skills of the pastor. The first chapter of this book, then, will offer a new configuration for parish leadership, one that is less dependent on a single person to determine whether the parish will be alive and grow or will remain content to serve the "regulars" who come to church but are unwilling to risk a future of new possibilities. First, however, a history of my involvement in parishes will give the context for what I propose in this book.

A Resource to Parishes

The Parish Evaluation Project (PEP) was initiated in 1973 with the intention of providing pastors, staffs and parish leaders with accurate information about the attitudes, needs and desires of the parishioners so that these leaders could make good plans for the future life of the parish. All too often the goals that the leadership constructed did not take into account the thoughts and feelings of the parishioners. PEP was founded to rectify that problem.

Over the years the Parish Evaluation Project process developed from a survey and visit to the parish at the beginning and end of a nine-month period to a longer involvement lasting more than two years. The original effort to survey parishioners' opinions remained, but we added weekend visits every six months that helped the parish leadership not only respond to people's needs, but address other issues as well. These included staff development, pastoral council formation, recruitment of volunteers, conflict management, outreach to inactive parishioners, to name but a few. Parishes did experience renewal. Committed and talented parishioners did join the leadership. Pastors and staffs did work more collaboratively together. But it became all too clear that when the pastor was changed, projects waned, structures collapsed, goals were left unattended. Seeing this, the Parish Evaluation Project tried to attack the core issue of how the change of pastors came about by providing a one-year process for the placement of pastors in parishes. With the help of Sr. Mary Benet McKinney, OSB, a transition process for pastors was developed that was used in three sample dioceses. In January, the pastors who were moving or retiring the following July gathered for a workshop to discuss how best to put closure to their pastorate and to prepare the parish and themselves for the coming transition. A parish transition team of staff, leaders and parishioners was assembled to shepherd the parish through the change. The team constructed a profile of the parish to be given to prospective pastors to assist them in their discernment about whether or not to apply for this parish. The intention was to find a good match of pastor and parish so that parish traditions and plans would not come to a halt with the arrival of a new pastor. (This process is spelled out in detail in *Changing Pastor*, which I co-authored with Mary Benet McKinney, OSB.)

The intention in designing this year-long process of pastoral transition was to influence the diocesan system of placement so that both the pastors and the parishes would not be at the mercy of a decision that was made with little or no input from them. Attending to the transition of pastors acknowledged that this person is at the center of parish life and operation. A change of pastor means a change of tone and personality for the parish as a whole. The heart, soul and head of the parish shifts when a new pastor is appointed, raising the questions: Is this the best way of operating? Is there an alternative? We feel there is. By entitling this book *The Parish as Covenant*, I want to signify that the promise and hope for a vital and alive parish community depends on a joint effort, a partnership, a mutual agreement, a system with more than just one person — the pastor — at its hub or center. More about this later. For now, a continuation of the story of how this came about.

Parish Assessment and Renewal

Along with the insights gained from addressing the transition of pastors came a fresh look at how best to work toward parish renewal. Were parishes encouraged to dig deeply to discover their core values, their purpose for existing? Were they inspired to step out of the mold and think creatively? Visiting a parish for a weekend every six months could not provide the concentration of time necessary for the renewal to take place. PEP spent too little time in the parish to make a lasting difference. Some other way of operating needed to be developed.

In 1998 a new model was put in place: the Parish Assessment and Renewal process, or PAR for short. At the heart of this model was a two-week, three-weekend visit to the parish by two members of the Parish Evaluation Project team. During the two weeks the team spent in the parish, it became saturated with the climate and culture of the parish community. This extended visit was preceded by three months of information gathering, including a survey of parishioners' attitudes and a notebook full of questions that the leaders answered as a help for locating the strengths and needs of each aspect of parish life and ministry. This new approach toward planning and renewal has been most successful, not only for the parishes involved but also for the insights and growth gained by the PAR team as well. Spending over two weeks in a parish, becoming immersed in its life and routine, experiencing the struggles and triumphs of ministry by the pastor, staff and leaders has resulted in a much better feel for the parish situation in a number of different settings. It is from this perspective that I offer the insights and suggestions contained in this book.

Fewer Priests

As Donald B. Cozzens argues in *The Changing Face of the Priesthood*, parishes are in trouble because the Catholic priesthood is in crisis. Under the present scheme, the pastor is at the center of the parish organization, which means everything funnels through him or her, whether coming from the bishop, diocesan offices or parish leadership. A few pastors may handle this situation quite well. They hand over decision making to staff members and parishioners. They delegate. They share responsibilities. They let go of the controls. They also balance their ministry with their personal lives so they are not worn out with the demands of the office. But this is a difficult mission to sustain and, as a result, a majority of pastors are becoming overwhelmed by the demands of the ministry and the rising expectations of the parishioners. These beleaguered pastors respond in one of two ways: Either they try to handle it all by themselves, working long hours and getting burned out and less effective in the process, or they withdraw and begin to function as if pastoring were more of a job than a ministry. They limit their interaction with parishioners. They do the minimum. It is not their fault. It is the way the system works (or doesn't work). By considering the pastor the sole head of the parish and the ultimate authority, the present system places a strangle hold on the local parish rather than being a liberating and holy experience for both pastors and parishioners.

The Catholic Church, especially in the United States, is in the midst of a profound transition. There are not enough priests to serve the People of God. Until there is a change in the requirements for ordination, the situation will only get worse. Parishes will get larger and larger, served by a single priest. The push to combine and cluster parishes will mount, to the chagrin of the parishioners who want to hold on to their own place of worship and their own locus of community. More and more parishes will have a reduced weekend schedule of Masses. Communion services will become more common. Non-ordained pastoral administrators will serve as pastors. Why is this happening? What is the Spirit trying to tell us?

Could it be that we are not yet ready for a change in the requirements for priesthood? We may have more lessons to learn. Too much is still

CHAPTER ONE

CHANGING THE SYSTEM:
FROM ONE FOCUS TO TWO

The parish priest is the proper pastor of the parish . . . he may
carry out the offices of teaching, sanctifying and ruling
with the cooperation of other priests or deacons and with the assistance
of lay members of Christ's faithful, in accordance with the law.

—CANON 519

A Clash of Two Systems

A gathering of pastors and parish staffs from a number of parishes was trying to clarify how and by whom important decisions were made. A religious sister offered the example of her own parish where she was the pastoral administrator. In effect, she was the pastor of the parish. The church was damaged beyond repair by a storm. Within twenty-four hours the decision was made to rebuild the church from the ground up. Who made this decision and how was it determined? The sister who was responsible for directing the parish said that it was not made by her or by any of the parish leaders. "It came from 'downtown,'" she said, "by those in control of the money." The group discussed this example for some time, wondering why no one in the parish community was even consulted. They all agreed that it was probably a good solution to rebuild the church, but it was not a collaborative effort. The sister, as it dawned on her what had happened, exclaimed, "What we have here is a clash of two systems."

One system was a top-down, hierarchical approach. It was efficient and immediate. "We will rebuild the church!" From this perspective the parish belonged to the diocese. Those "in charge" decided this would be the best thing to do. It gave the parishioners security, support and confidence that their church would be rebuilt, perhaps with a building even better than the one that was damaged. This efficient and immediate response, while reassuring, came with liabilities. It was a parenting approach that knew what was best for the parish. The people do not need to be asked. This system operates as a pyramid: Those in authority are at the top and those receiving "the benefits" are at the base.

In pastoring the parish, the religious sister had been trying to foster a more inclusive, consultative, circular model that had no top or bottom. Important decisions were made with a group of leaders only after consultation with the parishioners. The top-down pyramid system was in conflict with this inclusive circle model she was attempting to introduce in the parish. Most of the parishioners felt the rebuilding of the church was a good decision that needed to be made quickly. But suppose the diocese had said, "That storm was a clear sign from above that the parish needed to close and be merged with the neighboring church." Then the clash of the two systems would have been much more apparent. The people would have reacted immediately, exclaiming, "This is *our* church and we have a right to share in this decision."

Which system will win out? Both my intuition and experience tell me that an inclusive, participative system has a much better chance to succeed in our modern-day culture than a top-down, hierarchical one. People want to have a say in decisions that affect their lives and beliefs. They become more interested and involved if their wisdom, opinions and insights are enlisted, respected and acted upon. An approach from the top down may get the job done but it belongs to those who made the decision, not to those at the base of the pyramid. One example of this in a parish setting is the pastoral council that is only advisory to the pastor. The council gives advice and the pastor is free to act or not act on it. Most pastors say they always take the advice of the council and only in "very serious situations" would they choose to do otherwise. It sounds collaborative but it is a top-down model of "Father deciding." As council members often tell us, "Who wants to be part of that process? We have better things to do with our time than give ideas to the pastor. That is all it is, ideas, with little or no authority or ownership."

The Pastor at the Center

The rhetoric on the parish level is that the pastor is "one with the people." He is there to serve the parishioners. His wish is to work collaboratively with the staff and parish leadership. The reality is that the parish may look like it is operating as a collaborative, sharing model but the pastor is still at the center of the circle. All essential aspects of the parish go through him, as do the spokes of a wheel. He is the ultimate decider. This is what Canon Law stipulates. The difficulty is that in most situations it is not working.

The pastors are getting overworked and pulled in many directions at once. The pastoral staffs, which are comprised predominantly of women, are becoming frustrated with a collaborative model that is operating in name only. Parish leaders lose interest when they are not involved in the planning and decision making. Volunteer ministers lose patience when they must ask permission rather than being trusted to see a project through from beginning to end. Parishioners become angry when their views are not respected or consulted. Their anger turns to frustration when they see that nothing will change despite their protestations. They eventually become apathetic and withdraw their support and involvement as they lose heart trying to "buck the system."

In an attempt to change the parish system, the following diagram has been used with pastors and staffs, hoping to awaken a realization that the pastor does not always have to be in the center of the circle.

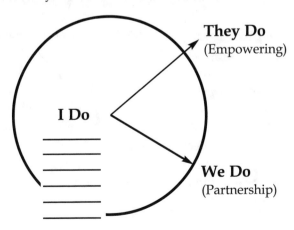

They Do
(Empowering)

I Do

We Do
(Partnership)

Figure 1-A: Shared Decision Making

After distributing this diagram to pastors and staffs, we ask them to list all the things that they do that no one else does. This is the "I Do" list. They might get advice or opinions from others, but it is their call, their task to decide. Each person talks over the list with someone else who knows the parish and how it operates. Are there any items on the "I Do" list that could be moved out of the center and shared with others in a partnership mode? Many pastors and staffs find the list to be a long one. They find themselves at the center of the ministry for which they are responsible. Others may be involved but the pastor or staff person is still the ultimate decider.

For example, one task of the pastor might be to lead the staff meetings. Is the pastor the only one willing and able to do this? Could it be shared with a few others on staff who would be equally as good at this task? Might it be shared with the entire staff on a rotating basis? The exercise of moving items out of the center of the circle is not always a simple one. It is one attempt, however, at changing the parish system from a top-down, inside-out model to more of a circular, shared model. As an extension of this exercise, the pastor and staff members are asked to move some of the items from the "I Do" list outside the circle to the "They Do" area. What are tasks that others could do with little or no involvement of the pastor or staff? This includes decision making as well as performing tasks and ministries. These people are both enabled and empowered for this responsibility by receiving training and credentials for the job, as well as full responsibility to do the task once they are trained. There may have to be clear lines of accountability and job descriptions attached to the task, but the pastor or staff person does not have to be involved, other than being informed that all is going well. This task is now off their plate of duties and responsibilities. One example, for instance, might be signing checks. In some parishes, this is still done by the pastor. It is a task that could easily be done by a business administrator or bookkeeper. Another example is a staff member in charge of pastoral care. Training people to be one-on-one caregivers is a necessary ingredient of this ministry, but does it have to be done by the staff person? Might it not be done just as well by experienced caregivers who could pair up with new recruits and do the training on the job?

The Team Approach Is Not Working

The attempt at pulling the pastor out from the center of the circle and placing the pastor on the rim with others who share the running and operation of the parish has had only limited success. Some places call this a *team* approach to pastoral ministry. The term is a tempting one. Everyone, pastor included, wants to be part of a team effort. But this notion can mean different things to different people. To some on staff or in leadership positions, this can mean sharing in the decision making and running the parish as a partnership. Each person has an area to attend to and a ministry to perform, but the "team" plans together the next steps, makes critical decisions in a consensus mode, and holds one another accountable for implementing tasks. To others, the team concept may have more of a sports connotation. Every team has a coach or captain. The group works together, but one person calls the plays or determines strategy. Only one person is "in charge" of the team. This ambiguity about team has led to frustration and misunderstandings, with many giving up on the attempt altogether.

An added detriment to this approach is that parishioners can get nervous with a team model. "Whom do I go to if I have a problem? Who really is in charge here? Where does the buck stop in this system?" Bishops and diocesan personnel also get nervous with the team concept because they don't know whom to contact if not the pastor. In one diocese, when the bishop invited the pastor in for a conference about a complaint he had received, the pastor showed up with the entire "team" of six people. "We make decisions as a whole, Bishop," the pastor said. "Whatever difficulty you have with me is shared by us all. We all agreed to the decision about which you received a complaint. We should all be here to talk about it and address your concerns."

Team ministry, in other words, is a lovely concept but it is not working in a system where the pastor is expected to be the ultimate authority. He is the one "in charge." So what to do? The hierarchical, top-down model is exclusive and arbitrary. The team model succeeds only occasionally when all the ingredients are in place. For most parish settings, however, it is an unrealistic approach. Is there another alternative? I believe a third option does exist, one that is a middle ground between one person being in charge and all persons, as part of a team, being in charge.

The Middle Ground

A lesson in solid geometry suggests a middle ground between one person in charge and the team approach. If a cone is sliced parallel to the base, a circle is created, as demonstrated in Figure 1-B.

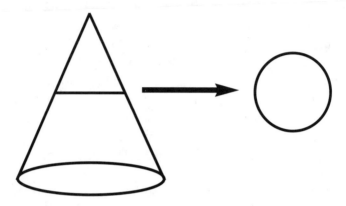

Figure 1-B: Generation of a Circle from a Cone

However, if a cone is sliced at an angle to the base, then an ellipse is created, as shown in Figure 1-C.

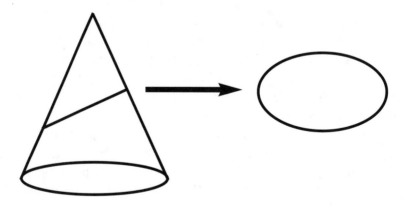

Figure 1-C: Generation of an Ellipse from a Cone

What is unique to an ellipse is that it does not have one focal point in the center as does a circle. It has *two* focal points, or foci, around which the ellipse is traced. (See Figure 1-D.)

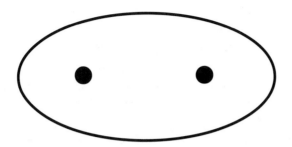

Figure 1-D: The Diagram of an Ellipse with Two Foci

There are examples of elliptical systems all around us. Our earth, for instance, follows an elliptical path around the sun. In family systems, the most healthy and balanced model is one in which both the husband and the wife share equally the decision making and management of the family. This healthy family system, in other words, has two focal points. In theater, both the director and the producer work together in creating a play. Each has a task to perform, but they operate as partners. Successful business corporations manifest this dual focus by having a Chief Executive Officer (CEO) and either a Chief Financial Officer (CFO) or Chief Operating Officer (COO). No one person is at the center of the corporation as the sole authority. If this can work in our physical world, in families and commerce, why not in the Church, at least on the parish level?

This dual focus system is already operating in some of the more successful models of American Catholic parishes. Two pastors introduced to each other at an intercultural conference of Catholic parishes near Mexico City struck up a conversation about the operation of their respective parishes. They both described a model in which they, as pastor, took care of the pastoral dimension, but left to a parish administrator all the physical, temporal, and personnel areas of parish life. They said, almost in unison, "Oh, I don't have anything to do with the running of the parish. I have this great administrator who takes care of all that! I don't know what I would do without her/him." These were pastors from parishes with a national reputation of being mega-parishes that attract parishioners from a large geographical area and a wide range of ages, especially young adults in their twenties and thirties.

These two very successful parishes have not one focus but two. People know to whom to go with a concern, either pastor or administrator. The system thrives as a partnership of two competent people running the parish, sharing both trials and triumphs. The pastors are not over burdened, despite the large number of parishioners. They are happy men, having served in this system for many years. Obviously, this system did not happen all by itself. These two pastors, each one being intuitive and self-confident enough to share the leadership of the parish, constructed this elliptical model of a parish with two centers. This elliptical model grew out of their willingness to trust the talents and capabilities of others.

These are not the only existing examples of this model. Many less well-known parishes operate this way, more out of necessity than by design. As one pastor said, "I was not ordained to be an administrator. Once I realized that this was not my gift, I found someone else to handle that aspect of the parish. Now she and I are happy as partners in ministry and the parishioners are much happier with this arrangement as well."

The question, of course, is whether it can survive when these gifted pastors are replaced. I believe it can if the system is accepted for what it is, an ellipse with two centers. The parish will change when the pastor is replaced, but the entire model will not collapse as often happens in a parish that has lost its single center for want of an adequate replacement. In the dual-focus system, when there is a change of pastors, the administrator remains in charge of the temporal affairs and directs this aspect of parish life and operation, leaving the new pastor free to concentrate on spiritual leadership and pastoral direction.

Once this new system takes hold, not only would the pastor be appointed by the diocese as a result of a well-developed process of transition, the administrator might be appointed by the diocese as well. The new person would be picked from a pool of well-trained, qualified administrators, all experienced in managing a modern Catholic parish and committed to working as partners in shared ministry with the pastor. Whenever a change of pastor or administrator takes place, much attention must be given to the leadership styles of both so that a good working relationship and sound partnership can be formed between the two.

A current example of a parish system with two focal points is one that does not have a resident ordained minister. Canon Law describes this situation by stating, "If, because of a shortage of priests, the diocesan bishop has judged that a deacon, or some other person who is not a priest, or a community of persons, should be entrusted with a share in the exercise of the pastoral care of a parish, he is to appoint some priest who, with the powers and faculties of a parish priest, will direct the pastoral care" (Canon 517, 2).

Such situations are becoming more and more common in the American Catholic parish scene. The most successful models are those in which the non-ordained pastoral administrator and the ordained sacramental minister operate as partners. This is most apparent at the weekend parish liturgies. The two people are present before the people at the Eucharistic ritual. Rather than confusing the congregation, this helps them realize that this is a joint effort of two people providing leadership in the liturgy. During the week, the administrator "pastors" the parish, usually in partnership with other staff and parish leaders. The priest is present for administering sacraments and the celebration of the Eucharist as needed, including weddings, anointings, reconciliation and funerals. The system, in other words, has two focal points: pastoral administrator and sacramental minister.

Another example of a dual-focus parish system is the pastoral council and pastor working in partnership. Canonically, the pastor is the "head" of the council. According to Canon 536, the pastoral council should be "presided over by the parish priest and have only a consultative vote." In practice, however, almost all pastoral councils have a chairperson who runs the meetings and sets up the agenda in consultation with the pastor. The more successful councils are joint efforts of pastor and leaders working in concert. When a difficult issue arises, the council does not deliberate while the pastor looks on from outside the group. Rather, the council members as a whole, with the pastor as one of them, share their wisdom and insights. They then come to a consensus as to what path to follow. The council is a single body, with the chairperson and the pastor working together as the two focal points of leadership.

Characteristics of a System

Because the word *system* has been used throughout this chapter, it would be helpful to discuss the characteristics of any system, whether a pyramid, circle or ellipse. A good way to symbolize a parish from a system's point of view is to picture a mobile hanging from the ceiling. The mobile consists of a number of objects balanced by sticks and string. If left undisturbed, it remains still. But move one part of that hanging mobile, and the whole system of interconnected parts begins to move.

So too with the parish system, or even the Catholic Church system as a whole. Move or change any one of the parts and the entire system will be affected. The Second Vatican Council is one example of a shift that changed how the Church functioned. But this event was preceded by smaller changes that prepared the way for the Council and put the system in motion. Examples include the Lord's Prayer which, while still said in Latin during Mass, was spoken out loud by the entire congregation. Catholics also began reading the Scriptures and forming discussion groups. Change one or other custom and the entire way of operating, top to bottom, begins to shift. This is how a system functions.

On a much smaller scale, change one aspect of parish leadership and the entire parish shifts. Suppose the principal of the school and the director of religious education decide to treat education of the children as a single entity. Each had been operating at the center of her own circle of ministry. They decide to combine forces and work as partners. No longer would the school and the religious formation program be separate but would become inter-related and inter-active. In making this change, the entire educational system shifts from two separate circles to one ellipse with two focal points, two co-leaders of a single system. This has a ripple effect throughout the parish. Soon the pastoral staff changes its way of interacting, as does the leadership of the parish as a whole. Change one piece of the system and the entire apparatus is in motion.

Consider the pastor who takes a risk and decides to share equally with the pastoral associate in the running and leadership of the parish. The two stand up before the congregation at all of the weekend Masses and suggest a new way of doing business and ministry in the parish, asking parishioners for their reaction. They refer the parishioners to the bulletin for a list of possible duties and issues that would relate to the pastor and ones that would relate to the pastoral associate. After a few weeks of listening to parishioners' comments, the pastor and pastoral associate decide to initiate the new way of operating. The pastor announces to the people, "We are going to give this a try. From now on, if you have a question or concern about one of the areas related to the associate's duties, don't come to me. She has full authority to handle the matter.

Don't worry, we are in constant contact with each other, operating as a partnership and sharing the load. We feel this is a better way to serve the parish community." In making this change, not only are all aspects of the parish system affected, so are the surrounding parishes and the diocese as a whole. Word gets around. Parishioners spread the story. Other pastors and staffs ask questions. Diocesan offices make note of this shift. Other places begin contemplating a similar move. Change one part of the system and the entire operation changes.

Work the Process

Because an entire system is affected, changes take time. With a mobile hanging from the ceiling, gently blow on one piece of it and the movement will be communicated, over time, to the opposite side of the mobile. But it does take time. So too with parish and Church systems. "Do not become discouraged," is the message for impatient staffs. "The seeds are planted and are being watered. They will sprout after you are gone. But grow they will."

In working with systems, it is best to manage the process rather than the individual. The music minister, for instance, is having difficulty with the organist. The person is playing too slowly and too loudly. He also takes any criticism or corrections very poorly. To terminate the person would be unfair and harsh treatment. Better to work the process. This might mean considering how *all* those playing the organ at the Masses are assigned, trained or held accountable. This had not been done before. A more effective process might suggest a meeting of all the organists, have them talk about their experience and encourage them to visit one another's liturgies to see how each person plays. They might even consider exchanging Mass times on occasion. This might force the "problem person" to reconsider that ministry or, under the best scenario, to change his habits. Work the process. In doing so, it is not just the individual causing the problem who is affected; rather, the entire system is improved.

In one particular parish, the pastor did everything in the parish, from setting up chairs to counting the money. Rather than telling the pastor to let go and give others a chance, we tried to change the parish structure by creating coordinating groups in various areas of ministry. The areas included worship, education, outreach, community life and administration. The next step was to have all the coordinating groups meet at the same time on the same night. The pastor was not physically able to attend them all. They had to function on their own. This new leadership process created vacuums and opportunities for those other than the pastor to become involved. He loved it. "People are finally signing up and helping out," he told us. "I could never get anyone to do it so I just did it myself." Little did he realize that they didn't sign up because he had all the bases covered already. It was a closed system.

Attend to the System's Culture

Catholic parishes are complex systems. Each one has its own way of operating, along with a unique set of underlying assumptions, values and traditions. One has to look closely, however, to discover this underlying "culture" of the parish. For example, if Thursday is the pastor's day off, everyone knows that life at the office will be more casual on that day. This is part of how the parish operates. Or there may be an unvoiced assumption that the grade school is the most important part of the parish. As a result, the school gets more money, attention and care than any other program. As one staff member said, "That is just the way things are around here." There may be a tradition of starting every council meeting with prayer, although it must never go for more than five minutes. This is part of the council's culture. One aspect of the parish culture may be that the people do not hold hands during the Lord's Prayer at 7:30 Mass on Sunday morning but do hold hands at the other liturgies. Another assumption may be that the Saturday evening Mass is always "dead'; nothing will ever bring it to life. These are some of the unwritten rules of the parish's culture.

Other deeper issues affect the culture as well: "If you want to join this parish staff, we presume that you profess a progressive understanding of church, one that favors inclusive language and social awareness." "A willingness to run for the pastoral council means accepting a consensus style of decision making in which there are no winners or losers." "Working in this parish office requires that nothing said at work is ever repeated outside these walls."

Attending to such underlying values and assumptions sometimes means stopping the regular routine of work long enough to look at the group's culture, see what it contains, and evaluate how it affects the daily operation of the organization. This includes acknowledging some of the rules and values the culture contains and how these affect the daily interaction of the members. The culture changes with the makeup of the group, but it has a surprising tenacity and longevity. "Bucking the system" often means challenging unwritten values and assumptions. It is no easy task and often means failure, at least in the short term.

Parish staffs can find strength in articulating their staff culture by constructing a set of ground rules that all members agree will govern their interaction and operation. Some examples include: Everyone has a responsibility to foster a climate of trust in the group. Speak your feelings to the whole group, not to a few in the parking lot after the meeting. Start and end on time, except when all agree the meeting should go longer. Everyone has wisdom to share, no one person's wisdom is more important than another.

If the group, whether staff, council or committee, spends time trying to articulate the system's culture, its members will have a much better grasp of what drives the system and what makes the group function as it does. Members will also have a better chance of changing the system if they are able to name its underlying culture. Each parish, for instance, takes the rituals, regulations and directives of the Church and diocese and applies them to the culture of its own parish community. The rules are upheld but are interpreted differently depending on the inclination of the leaders and the people. Canon Law, for instance, asserts that the council is "presided over" by the pastor. But how that prescription is carried out in practice depends on the underlying culture of each parish.

Our contention is that it is possible to shift the predominant culture of American Catholic parishes from the pastor being the one, ultimate focus and primary decision maker of the parish to a shared ownership of the pastor and at least one other person as a dual focus of leadership. In this climate, staff members and parish leaders develop partnerships with one another as well. This change of system makes sense not only for the present situation but if and when the underlying culture of the institutional Church changes and returns to an ordained priesthood that includes both married and celibate candidates. When this happens and a pastor has family obligations beyond parish duties, then perhaps the running of a modern parish as a joint effort will become commonplace. Better that this system be put into place now rather than waiting until the Church changes the requirements of the priesthood.

suggestion that Church may change requirements of priesthood

A Tension Between Group and Individual Goals

Important aspects of any system is that changing one part will eventually change the whole; changing the entire system takes time; that it is better to work the process than to criticize the individual; and that every system has a culture of unwritten, underlying values and ways of operating. Another characteristic of a well-functioning system is that there is a healthy tension between the goals, vision and direction of the whole and those of individual members. Whenever a person joins a staff and is willing to be part of the staff system, he or she is caught in a dilemma: "How much do I give up of my own desires and dreams for this parish or staff in order to 'fit in' around here? How much do I hang on to my own aspirations and insist that the staff make room for my own individuality, my unique gifts and insights?" This struggle contributes to the health of the staff because it keeps it interdependent, rather than a collection of independent individuals, each operating apart from the whole, or a group of followers, all dependent on the wishes of the pastor or some other dominant individual on staff.

This is one characteristic of a healthy system that is often missing in the present parish culture. The pastor is at the center of the circle, the hub of the wheel. His voice and views predominate and the healthy tension of "give and take" is lost. A much better configuration is a system that fosters a balance between essential aspects of parish life. This includes a balance between pastoral ministry and administration, between care of the parishioners and reaching out beyond parish boundaries to care for others in need, between educating children and focusing on adult formation, between fostering private devotions and stressing communal worship. Again, a dual focus has a better chance of maintaining this balance of personal goals and group directions. Changing the local parish system might even affect other aspects of the larger Church culture as well. Every change in the system affects the whole.

Maintaining Permeable Boundaries

Finally, a system that is alive and has a promising future is one in which the boundaries are open and permeable. Disastrous examples of closed systems are all too common. On the extreme end of the spectrum, the tragic results of closed religious sects that end in mass suicides illustrate the dangers of a closed system that does not have permeable boundaries.

On a parish level, the group that subtly closes out membership starts feeding upon itself and consumes its own resources. The Holy Name Society or Women's Club that wonders why it can't get any younger members is experiencing the result of closing the gates to the forces of change and becoming a clique or group unto itself. A council that is self-contained and has little influence in the parish wonders why no one knows it exists or wants to run as a candidate. A youth group that caters to just one style of activity or clientele has difficulty with maintaining an attractive image. A charismatic renewal prayer group that has little to do with the mainstream of the parish wonders why it is on the margin of the parish community. The boundaries surrounding these groups are well defined. Much of the energy of each group is used up in protecting its identity from outside forces and shielding its members from becoming "contaminated."

If, on the other hand, a system is open to the surrounding environment and forces of change, if it stays alert to aspects of the larger society that affect its operation, then it will remain alive and healthy. If the group has a purpose beyond itself so that it is not self-serving, the organization will discover new energy to fuel its activity. The irony is that a system that "circles the wagons" and tries to protect its own interests will eventually die. On the other hand, a system that keeps giving of itself and spends its energies outside of itself finds the life and energy to grow to new heights. This is a systems approach to the Gospel axiom, "the one who loses his or her own life will gain it."

Steps for Changing the System

Changing the parish system is not easy. There has been a long tradition of everything depending on the pastor as the central focus of the parish. Shifting this system to a dual focus, one in which the operation and direction of the parish is shared with at least one other person, will require some intermediate steps.

The first step is to locate existing models of an elliptical parish and study them to see how they operate. Examples do exist in most dioceses. These are places where, because of the urging of the pastor, the press of circumstances or the giftedness of one or more staff members, at least one other person besides the pastor is given the authority and legitimacy to share the running of the parish as co-leader with the pastor. The titles associated with this person will vary. In one place it may be the pastoral associate; in another, the parish administrator or parish director. The title is not as important as the image that this person commands among the leaders and the people. The parish system revolves around two people: the pastor and this other individual. Each has a sphere of influence and a defined set of duties and responsibilities. In some cases, the duties may overlap. In other situations, it is clear that only one of the two is the contact person. That is the one who decides or directs this particular area or aspect of parish life.

A common example in parishes that have a school is the interdependency of the pastor and the principal. Both have a sphere of activity that the other respects and affirms. There is no sense calling the rectory if one's child is going to miss a day of school. There is no need calling the school office if one wants to schedule a baptism or wedding. A less common situation is that parish in which an administrator is in charge of all temporal affairs of the parish, including security, maintenance, scheduling, finances, personnel and staff development. The pastor stays away from these issues and, as a result, has more time and energy to lead and direct the pastoral, sacramental and spiritual aspects of the parish.

How does this come about in Catholic parishes? Is this co-leader of the parish hired by the pastor or by the pastoral council or by some other body? What happens when there is a change of pastors? Do the people who remain have any assurance that the system of a dual focus will continue? Will the reputation of this unique way of running a parish be strong enough so that when the diocese assigns a new pastor, this person will be able and willing to work within this framework? These are as yet unanswered questions. Many examples of this type of parish system need to be observed closely to see whether they can endure pastoral transitions and whether they will become more common as an accepted model for Catholic parishes in the future. If your own parish is considering such a move, visit others that have a reputation of shared leadership and see how they do it.

A second step in the direction of establishing a dual focus is to look within the parish itself and discover what areas of ministry exhibit a shared leadership or dual-focus approach. Some staff members are better at this than others. When they work with parish leaders or other staff members, there is an equal ownership manifested in the sharing of decisions and planning. Two staff members, or a staff person and the head of a committee, share responsibilities and authority in common. The ministry has a dual focus.

On the other hand, parish staffs complain about having to work in a hierarchical, top-down environment. Often, however, it is these same complainers who also operate out of an authoritarian style of leading themselves. Committee members and volunteers end up being "go-fors" and implementers of the staff person's projects rather than joint planners and co-owners of the task. What is intended and what actually happens do not always match.

Examples of co-leadership might include the liturgist and the music director, the principal and the assistant principal, the pastoral-care director and the head of the outreach committee, the director of religious education and the youth minister, the pastor and the chair of the pastoral council. It is a joint effort. Neither one is "in charge." Both work hand in hand as equals in this ministry. It is a special gift to be able to let go enough to share the power and responsibility with another person, but it is happening in many unheralded and creative ways. Watch for these within the parish. Celebrate and affirm them when they do occur. Use them as models for other aspects of parish life or even for the parish system as a whole.

Envision Options—Try It Out

A third step toward creating a "dual-focus" parish is to become more conscious of what options are possible. Provide opportunities for staff, leaders and people to talk about what would be the advantages and disadvantages of this approach. Envision how this might happen in the current situation, given the personalities, gifts and inclinations of the pastor, staff members and parish community. Try it out in subsections of the parish to see how it functions. For example, rather than having a chair and a vice-chair on the pastoral council or finance council or school board, consider having co-chairs. Two people are discerned or selected for leading the group. They share the task as equals. They both might help make up the meeting's agenda. They could take turns running the meeting, one chairing the meeting one month, the other the next. Afterwards they could give feedback to each other about how the meeting could be improved or help the group reflect at the end whether everyone's wisdom was listened to and shared. Not only would this take the load off of one person's shoulders for leading all the meetings, it makes for a more productive, high quality meeting as well. People are much more likely to volunteer to be a leader if they know that they can do this in partnership with another person.

Once various attempts at a dual focus are tried, they need to be evaluated within a set period of time, perhaps six to nine months. Catholic parishes are notorious for ignoring this evaluation piece. A decision is made and it then becomes set in stone, which is not a good way of proceeding. Better to build into the system a prearranged time to ask, "What is working and why? What is not working and why? What changes are necessary? Should we continue on this path or should we try out another option?" This tradition of regular evaluation will contribute to a more healthy and productive way of acting. This is especially important in trying out a new system or way of operating.

Finally, once a comfortable model of shared ownership and dual responsibility is discovered, spread the word. Make it known. Keep it visible. Tell the world or at least inform the parishioners, neighboring parishes, the diocese and the bishop. Parishioners especially need to be encouraged to see the benefits of this new, open, shared system. Tell them what is being done and why. Be up front about what this new system makes possible that could not be accomplished before it was adopted. Clarify whom to see for what issues and concerns under the new system, how it operates and where the focus of decision making lies in each particular situation. Too often good systems of shared ownership and partnership are kept secret. Insiders and outsiders alike have only vague ideas that this place is different, but they are not sure how or why. Establish the reputation that this parish has a dual focus. "The pastor is not the only one in charge here. Do not call him if you want a door opened. He does not have all the keys anymore." Get the message out to the diocese, "Do not send all that diocesan mail to the pastor. He is not the one who should see it. It will only get thrown away."

By establishing a strong reputation of shared ownership, the parish has a better chance of surviving intact whenever there is a transition of pastors. Clergy, diocesan personnel and the bishop all know what to expect and are therefore more likely to respect the way the parish operates in assigning a replacement for the current pastor. This, however, could uncover two different systems at work: the diocesan placement process and the local parish configuration. If the parish does not work at creating a positive reputation of shared leadership, it could well be at the mercy of receiving someone as pastor who is not only unfamiliar with the system but also antithetical to its intent. This would be a great loss to the parish and a waste of creative energy. Be pro-active in communicating this partnership model to the bishop and diocese, showing how beneficial it is to both the leadership and the people. This might even change aspects of the diocesan system as a whole.

A Covenant Relationship

There is more at stake here than a change of systems. God said to Noah, "As a sign of this everlasting covenant which I am making with you and all living beings, I am putting my rainbow in the clouds. It will be the sign of my covenant with the world" (Genesis 9:12–13). Yahweh also entered into a covenant with Abraham and Sarah. Together they fostered a new nation, a Chosen People. The God of the Burning Bush entered into partnership with Moses and Aaron to set the Jewish people free. It was a joint effort. Jesus preached a leadership of mutuality. "Do not lord it over others," was his mandate. Perhaps something new and exciting is on the horizon. The focus of the chapters that follow is to spell out ways that a pastoral partnership approach could come into being and become operative in the local parish.

An Example of Dual-Focus Leadership
As Manifested by the Leaders and People of
Pax Christi Catholic Community, Eden Prairie, Minnesota
By
Gerald P. Roth, Parish Director

Pax Christi Catholic Community was founded in 1981 in Eden Prairie, a suburb of Minneapolis. By the time I joined the staff in 1989 as the parish administrator, or as we call it, the parish director, the parish had grown to over 2,600 households and was completing a second building expansion. The guiding principle of the parish is that the People of God are the Church, which is exemplified by shared leadership and collegial involvement. In that context, the pastor, or as we call him, the pastoral director, and myself share the dual role of leaders of the Catholic Community. The Pax Christi Community booklet describes this relationship. "Our Pastoral Director (pastor) and Parish Director (administrator) share the responsibility to implement the vision of the Community. That vision encompasses an atmosphere where staff and Community members can mirror the creativity of the God who seeks expression in each of us. We commit ourselves to keeping that partnership."

Leadership in the Pax Christi Community comes from many sources. The strength of the Community is the involvement of hundreds of members leading the multiple functions of the Community in innumerable ways. The Community Council (pastoral council) looks to two key individuals for energy and initiative in implementing future directions set by the Council. These two positions are the pastoral director (pastor) and parish director (administrator) who, in turn, report to the Community Council and receive feedback as to how they are carrying out their leadership positions.

For the last six years, the two directors, the pastor and myself, have created a working partnership. As with any organization in today's world of rapid change, the two of us have been challenged on many fronts. The secret to managing change is to remain a lifelong learner, and so, over the years we have identified and adopted several key principles that have allowed our partnership to flourish.

An honest recognition of each other's strengths and weaknesses: One example of this is the recently completed six-million-dollar addition to our facility. Throughout the design and construction phase that lasted several years, the project was led by myself with a team of staff and Community members. The pastoral director (pastor) had no accountability on this project. As a member of the Community Council (pastoral council), the pastoral director was informed of the progress of the project and participated in key decisions affecting funding and authorization to complete the project. He frequently sites this project as an example of how the dual-leadership model has allowed him to focus on the pastoral health of the Community while other critical operations continue under the leadership of the parish director.

Regular and honest communication between the two directors: In any group where two people share leadership, there is a risk of trying to divide the leadership in order to gain an advantage. Staff or members of the Community may ask one of the directors for a decision affecting Community operations. If the response is not supportive of their position, they approach the other leader to see if the original response can be challenged. Through frequent communication, the two directors rely on a collective wisdom for decision making while avoiding the dangerous triangulation affect that can paralyze and divide a community.

Belief in the wisdom of subsidiarity and delegation: Even with two directors, the workload of pastoral leadership can be overwhelming. Subsidiarity suggests that decisions should be made and activities directed by members of the organization who have the information, skills and authority to create a successful outcome. One example is the Manager of Building Services who has full authority to direct the operations of her department. The manager hires staff, contracts for services, purchases maintenance supplies and manages building and grounds operations within the parameters of an annually approved budget. Little or no input is required from either the two directors.

Trust and mutual respect of one another: This principle forms the backbone of an effective and fulfilling partnership. The words, actions and decisions of each director must exhibit a commitment to each other's success. Canon

Law clearly prescribes that full authority for parish operations resides solely with the pastor (pastoral director). For a dual-leadership model to work in a parish organization, it is imperative that the pastor willfully shares that authority with his leadership partner (parish director). This sharing is based on an honest assessment of each other's gifts and a trust-filled working relationship that maximizes each other's strengths and minimizes each other's weaknesses. From the beginning of this dual-leadership model, Fr. J. Timothy Power (pastoral director) has consistently recognized the gifts that I, as the parish director, have brought to the growing Community of Pax Christi. He has encouraged me to creatively use these gifts in service to Pax Christi's ministries and members. Rather than diminish his role, Fr. Power has frequently commented on how the dual-leadership model has enhanced his ability to perform his pastoral duties. Because of this trust-filled working relationship, the two directors are able to have honest discussions about difficult operational issues. The blend of pastoral and organizational analysis brings a collective wisdom to the human personnel, financial or ministerial decisions required in the daily activity of my position as the parish director.

In reviewing the nineteen-year history of Pax Christi, it is clear that the dual-leadership model emerged as a natural response to a growing and complex faith community. The conditions for its success include a trusting pastor, as well as creative leaders who are willing to embrace change and allow the Pax Christi Catholic Community to continually be refashioned as an organization that can provide a broad array of ministries for its growing membership. Margaret Wheatley wrote in *Leadership and the New Science*, "How will we navigate these times? The answer is, together. We need each other differently now. We cannot hide behind our boundaries, or hold onto the belief that we can survive alone. We need each other to test our ideas, to share what we're learning, to help us see in new ways, to listen to our stories. We need each other to forgive us when we fail, to trust us with their dreams, to offer their hope when we've lost our own."

(Pax Christi Catholic Community is located at 12100 Pioneer Trail, Eden Prairie, Minnesota 55347. The phone number is 952-941-3150. Their e-mail address is pax@paxchristi.com)

CHAPTER TWO

PASTORING A MODERN PARISH: NOT ONE BUT MANY

I have grasped you by the hand;
I formed you,
And set you as a covenant
of the people.

— ISAIAH 42:6

For the season of Lent in the year 2000, Bishop Kenneth Untener of the Diocese of Saginaw, along with a few other people, put together a "Black Book." It contained a reflection for each day of Lent using the Passion according to St. Mark. The booklet was given to every parishioner of the diocese with the encouragement to pray for six minutes every day using the passage from the booklet. It provided a unified effort throughout the diocese of prayer and reflection during Lent. The booklet became so popular that individuals, parishes and even entire dioceses requested copies. The bishop and the "Little Books" committee, as they called themselves, decided to publish a "Blue Book" for the following Advent, and a "White Book" for the Easter season.

This is an example of good pastoring, providing the tools and resources, encouragement and challenge that will empower others to grow in their faith and to participate in the pastoring effort. Good pastoring is not up to the pastor alone. It is a joint effort of pastor and pastoral administrator, of staff members and pastoral council, of leaders and people.

Good Pastoring

Good pastoring happens when a pastoral council sits down for an evening meeting and begins to reflect on what direction the parish should take for the coming year. "What should be our theme for the coming year?" the leader asks. Council members have gathered information about how the current theme of "Joining Hands Outside Our Circle" has taken hold in the parish. Has any progress been made in breaking down barriers between groups, in opening up the in-groups, in welcoming newcomers, in inviting inactive Catholics back to church, in reaching out to other churches and those of other faiths? The evening turns into a lively discussion as people tell stories and give witness about how the parishioners have come together as a community over the past year. Much more needs to be accomplished but great steps have been taken. There is not enough time at the meeting to think up a new theme for the coming year but council members leave the meeting feeling affirmed and graced in their ministry of leadership.

Good pastoring happens when the liturgy coordinating group calls together the presiders and key liturgical ministers to reflect on the Holy Week and Easter services just completed. The co-chairs of the group lead them through an evaluation of each day's ritual. Were people touched by the experience? Did the liturgies flow easily? Was there a chance for both personal and communal prayer? Did each service stay within reasonable time limits, not wearing out the congregation but not rushing or feeling pressured to end "on time"? Were the liturgies prayerful experiences that moved people to greater bonding and service in their lives, or were they more like shows that people watched but with little application to their daily lives? Each aspect of the rituals, from music to hospitality, from presiding to proclaiming were analyzed and suggestions made for changes in next year's services. This is an example of pastoring as a joint effort.

Good pastoring happens when the pastoral staff plans an overnight away from the parish to pray together and to reflect on their ministry. Each member of the staff contributes to the success of the two-day outing that includes time for individual prayer, communal faith sharing, evaluation of ministries and establishing goals for the coming year. Time is set aside for fun, frolic and good food. It is a celebration of their common task of pastoring a modern parish.

Good pastoring happens when the pastoral administrator, along with the finance council, makes a presentation at the Masses about parish spending for the past year. It shows how the contributions that the parishioners have made were used for adult formation, outreach to the needy, music for the liturgy, a service project to Mexico and a parish mission during Lent. The sharing of people's lives and livelihood have been multiplied and expanded through parish ministries and projects. It is no longer just dollars and cents that have been contributed but a means for helping and healing others. The presentation at the end of each of the weekend liturgies is greeted with applause and acclaim for all the parish has done to not bury the talents (contributions) of the people but to put them to good use.

Most of all, good pastoring includes the pastor, or the person who takes the place of the pastor as pastoral administrator. His or her task, in providing leadership, is twofold. The person must be both the *bearer of the dream* and the *instigator of change.* In the change of system considered here there would be a dual focus of not just the pastor alone as leader but at least two people who would share the load and responsibility of pastoring. At the same time, the designated pastor does play a critical role in keeping the vision and dream of what the parish *could be* before the minds and hearts of the leaders and the people. This is not, however, just the pastor's dream. It is a shared vision of many people about what the future could be, and all that must be accomplished in the parish to realize this future.

Suppose the dream of the staff and leaders is a dual responsibility of the pastor and the administrator leading the parish. They see the wisdom in such an arrangement and seek to locate an administrator who could handle this job. The staff and leaders also realize that they will have to adjust their own expectations so that the pastor is no longer the only focus of all that goes on in the parish. The pastor's job is to keep that vision before the consciousness of the leaders and the people and not to let it die. It was, however, a dream of the entire leadership, not just the pastor's idea. Once a suitable administrator is found and hired, the pastor needs to adjust people's perceptions of joint pastoring so that the administrator is recognized as an equal partner in leadership and not just a "go-for" for the pastor.

This leads to the second aspect of good leadership: being an instigator of change. Although many people participate in the pastoring of the parish, part of the pastor's role is to keep challenging parishioners to grow in an awareness of God's call to greater freedom and holiness. The pastor

keeps urging the people not to settle for the *status quo* or to become compla-
cent with what *is* rather than seeking for what *could be*. Others on the staff
and in leadership positions also participate in this impetus for change.

One reason parishes lose their edge and fail to respond to changing
needs and new directions is because they become comfortable and secure
in the present way of operating. The business world has witnessed many
companies that failed because they were not able to adjust to changing
markets, products and resources. So too with the parish. The leader's role
is to keep pushing the limits, stretching the boundaries, seeking alternatives. That is what Jesus did and the Jewish establishment grew angry. In
between the lines of the Gospel, one senses the leaders saying to Jesus, "How
dare you tell us what to do. Why are you doing these acts that threaten our
way of operating and our leading of the people?" This, however, did not
dampen Jesus' challenge to their unjust and oppressive practices.

Some pastors have been able to challenge the staff and leaders to formulate creative dreams for the parish, to keep these dreams present in the
minds of the parishioners and thereby change people's way of thinking
and acting. These pastors have also been able to spread out their leadership and share it with others. They are not the only bearers of the dream
or the only instigators of change. It becomes a joint effort. It does take
someone, however, to get it started. This person does not have to be the
pastor. It could be the administrator, the pastoral associate, a member of
the parish staff or a key leader in the parish, someone willing and able to
motivate people to move from what is to what could be.

Setting a Collaborative Tone

Consider the parish that is undergoing a change of pastors. The current pastor is about to retire. He has been a good pastor over the last
twelve years, but in recent years some of the ministries and projects have
not been kept up to date. Parishioners have grown accustomed not to
expect too much from the liturgies or from the pastoral care of the pastor.
He is well liked, even endearing to the parishioners, but whatever changes
and new growth are likely to happen must await a change of pastors.

Eventually a new pastor is appointed. He arrives, assuring people
that he has not come with his own agenda or vision. He wants to listen and
hear what people want and desire. This, in itself, is a change. As soon as
the new pastor says hello and begins greeting people and paying attention

to their needs and desires, a change of tone happens. It feels to the congregation as if a lid has just been taken off the parish. New and wonderful options might now be possible. It is not so much *what* he says but the *way* he says it, with both conviction and energy. He emphasizes that the parish belongs to the people, not to him. It is a refreshing and welcomed change. This is an example of one essential of good pastoring, to *set the tone* of shared vision, participative leadership and common ownership. In the words of one pastor, "This is not *my* parish. It is *our* parish, yours and mine together. It is up to all of us to make it work."

When a change of pastor occurs, the personality and culture of the parish changes. It can be a sudden change or a slow, more subtle shift of emphasis. Eventually the tone of the liturgies, the direction of the staff, the agenda of the council meetings, the emphasis on outreach to the needy, the use of parish funds: all are influenced by the personality, values and desires of the new pastor. If the new pastor's tone is one of partnership and shared ownership, then it is possible that the parish system can change from a single to a dual focus as suggested earlier. Perhaps this change does take place and a person is found to work as a partner with the new pastor. The inclination of the new pastor becomes the dream of the parish. People begin to catch on that "we are in this together. It is up to *us* and not just the pastor to make this parish successful and to become a place that everyone can call home."

Slowly the style and operation of the parish shifts. "I want this parish," the pastor says, "to be a joint effort of all of us. We are in this together and for the long haul. I cannot do it alone. I choose to work in partnership with the new parish administrator as a model that this entire parish is a joint effort of holiness and service. The two of us have agreed to enter into a covenant relationship with each other and with God to make this happen. Come, be part of this bright new future of shared ownership."

In fostering this new emphasis and direction, the pastor is calling the leaders and the people to a new reality. This tone-setting is a mark of good pastoring. It is visionary as well as concrete and practical. Robert Coles, in his *Lives of Moral Leadership,* tells the story of interacting with Senator Robert Kennedy in the struggle to feed undernourished children in southern United States. The senator was convinced of the need, even visiting families and gaining firsthand knowledge of their plight. But he was also a savvy politician who knew how to work the system of compromise in order to move his proposal of food stamps through Congress. So, too, with good pastoring.

If a parish wishes to continue operating out of a partnership model, then the pastor and leaders will have to work at creating a positive reputation of a dual-focus parish in the diocese. Then, when it is time to appoint a successor to the current pastor, the bishop and diocesan personnel will be sensitive to the unique culture and style of this parish. Good pastoring, in other words, is thinking ahead to future contingencies and not just the current situation. The person who shares the dual focus with the current pastor must be given assurance that her or his job will not come to an end or be reconfigured once a new pastor is assigned. The hope is that in those parishes where the pastoring role and running of the parish are shared with at least one other person, that a change of pastors will not constitute a radical shift in the tone and culture in the parish. Hopefully, the transition will be less disruptive than in the typical model of the pastor being the only person in the center of the parish operation. Only one of the two leaders is being changed. The one who remains helps maintain continuity.

Nevertheless, the assigned pastor, even in a dual-focus parish, has a profound effect on the life, tone and direction of the parish. That is an advantage for pastors whose tone is one of shared ownership and partnership. They can create this tone among leaders and people because of the influence they have for effecting change.

The possibility for a shift to a shared leadership model becomes more likely when there is a change from an ordained pastor to a pastoral administrator. The parish no longer has a resident priest as pastor. A priest comes in on weekends to preside at the liturgies. The pastoral administrator becomes, in the effect, the new pastor.

The tone set by most pastoral administrators is that the parish belongs to the people. They may be the assigned leader, but to make the place work, everyone has to take part. Parishioners respond for a number of reasons. For one thing, they tend not to put the administrator on a pedestal as they might an ordained pastor. People also feel the urgency to make this new configuration work. If it doesn't, the parish might close. They might also feel sorry for the administrator and are more willing to help the pastoral administrator to a greater extent than if a priest were the pastor. Whatever the reason, the tone of co-ownership and joint leadership is generally stronger in the parishes that do not have an ordained priest as pastor.

Whether the parish is led by a priest or a pastoral administrator, setting a tone of shared leadership captures people's imaginations and elicits their involvement and ownership. More than all the presiding at liturgy or ministry that a pastor does, setting the tone can make the difference. People respond when the pastor says to the parishioners, "This is not *my* parish. This is *our* parish. We all have joint ownership. We can accomplish great things together. Pastoring is not something I do alone. We do it together. Join me in this exciting adventure! There is no telling what God's graces can accomplish among us as one community, working together in a covenant relationship."

Leading Rather than Managing

Good pastoring must include a mixture of both leading and managing, but with a greater proportion of leading rather than managing. Leading helps a group or parish determine where it wants to go, what will be its vision and future. Once the desired outcome is determined, then managing is the combination of all that is needed to get to that end.

In a research project we conducted to determine how pastors spent their time, we asked six groups of pastors in six different parts of the country to keep track of their time for a given week. Where did they spend most of their time? The highest time user was liturgy, both preparing for and presiding at Eucharist. A close second, however, was in administrative duties, handling the daily routine of paper work, personnel issues, upkeep and scheduling. This is not what priests were ordained to do. They were called to be leaders rather than managers.

In a series of workshops for clergy of a particular diocese, they were divided into two groups. One set was for those priests who were about to be assigned to their first pastorate; the other set was for those who had just completed their first year as a new pastor. The issues, questions and concerns for each group could not have been more different. Those about to be pastors were concerned about parish vision, about what the parish was supposed to become and how they could help that happen, about staffing issues and working with others. The concerns of the second group, those already pastors, were almost entirely administrative. How to get bids for new construction, how to keep parish buildings in good shape, how best to bank the money, how and when to fire a problem employee.

These administrative details, while important, can be a waste of a pastor's skills and abilities. All the more reason to move toward a dual-focus parish system. Someone else, other than the pastor, should be authorized to handle the administrative and personnel issues. This frees the pastor to lead, to be the bearer of Gospel values and spiritual dreams in the parish. It allows the pastor to be the instigator of change for a new way of being a parish and to be aware of and responsive to the needs of those within the parish and those in the surrounding area.

One pastor was a great dreamer but an incompetent administrator. Anytime the pastor went on vacation or took a break, the staff got worried. He would return with grandiose plans for the parish. On one occasion, he showed me around an old warehouse a few blocks from the church. He wanted to make it into a roller-skating rink for the youth and young families. All the staff could do was shake their heads. "Just another one of his pipe dreams," they would lament. The rink never got built. What the parish really needed, however, was a bigger church building. For this project the pastor became a true leader. He called out the best in people, stretching their imaginations about what their worship space could be and how it could help the parish community pray and worship together. *How* it was to happen was not his concern, just *that* it would happen. His pastoral leadership will last far beyond his stay in the parish, manifested in the worship space he helped create as a joint effort with the people.

Another pastor exercised good leadership by asking the parishioners what they wanted in renovating the church. It no longer could accommodate the numbers now attending Mass. The overwhelming response was, "Whatever you do, don't destroy the lovely *feel* of our church. Don't make it so modern that we won't recognize it as a church." With the help of a creative architect and input from the congregation, a new plan was accepted that turned the church completely around; the back was now the front and the front the back. This allowed for the same *feel* of the original church but made room for new expansion. It also included a gathering space where people could socialize before and after Mass. The pastor manifested good leadership by listening well to people's needs, finding qualified people who could translate needs into action, and calling people to joint ownership in the project.

Managing the Image

The pastor, in partnership with others, is meant to lead. The pastor must also manage some aspects of parish life. One important area is managing how the pastor is present to the parish community. A helpful exercise is to ask the pastor to write down words that describe the image of how he sees himself in the parish. The list might include such words as *available, friendly, resourceful, prayerful.* Then the pastor is asked to write down words he feels that someone on staff or on the council might use to describe his image. This often becomes a different set of words, even when constructed by the pastor. The list might include *impatient, hurried, controlling, in charge, unavailable.*

People will size up a pastor quickly, forming an image that may be wide of the mark from what the pastor either desires to hear or is aware of about himself. One essential for good pastoring is to work on creating a positive image. This applies to the pastor, to the parish administrator, to the staff, to the pastoral council, to any group in pastoral leadership.

The first step toward managing a positive image is to pay attention to high-impact areas of pastoring and leadership. Much of pastoring is relation-building. As a result, a good way to fashion a positive image is to devote time to activities and rituals that involve relating to key groups and individuals. One pastor, in an effort to get to know and listen to a cross-section of parishioners, held a Sunday afternoon social once a month for a random group of parishioners. People were personally invited according to when they had registered in the parish. One month might be for all those who joined one to three years ago, another for those who had been members for fifteen to twenty years. He called it "Rap with Fr. Ray." Babysitting was provided, as were simple refreshments. People sat around in a circle and said whatever was on their minds as he listened. This created an image throughout the parish that this pastor was interested in each one of them, not in a select group of "old timers" or the "high money givers."

Another pastor was skilled at creating the image of being present at parish meetings and functions. He knew when to be present at just the time that was most appropriate. He did not always remain for the entire session, but people appreciated his presence nonetheless. This is one way of managing his presence in the parish.

Some priests or staff members have an ability to be present before and after the weekend Masses in such a way that manifests their availability and interest in the people. Other pastors may be present but they do not create the same positive image because they do not show the same interest and connection with people. Good pastoring—and this is not directed just to the pastor—means knowing how to be present and how to manage a positive image.

Clarifying the Decision Making

Good pastoring can be greatly enhanced by the C-D-I of decision making. It is a simple concept but profound in its application. C stands for Consult, D for Decide and I for Inform. Make a list of recent decisions that were made in the parish. These might include changing the Mass schedule, renovating a building, buying new hymnals, choosing a new religious education program, resurfacing the parking lot, twinning with a poor parish, having a "welcome home" weekend for inactive Catholics, to name but a few.

Then identify the persons who were the actual deciders for each situation and those who would be the *best* persons to be the deciders if the issue came up today. Sometimes the actual and the ideal were the same, but many times they were not. Who, for instance, should decide the change in the Mass schedule? Why is there even a need for a change? The answer to the second question might be that the parish is losing the ordained associate pastor and only one priest will be available for Masses. The parish will have to go from five Masses to three on the weekend. That is a *given* because, according to diocesan guidelines, the pastor can preside at only three Masses on the weekend. But who decides what the new schedule will be? The pastor? The staff? The pastoral council? The liturgy committee? The parishioners? Too often the response comes back like a Greek Chorus, "The pastor!" At which point the pastor cries out, "Why me?"

Suppose, in a given parish, it is the liturgy committee that is to decide about the weekend Mass schedule. Good pastoring means that they do not make the decision in isolation. They consult the parishioners (C), at least those who attend church on the weekends. They also consult the pastor, the staff, and the liturgical ministers. The committee puts out a brief survey of possible times as a way of consulting the people's opinions. The committee, however, explains that this is *not a vote*. A majority will not decide this question. This is merely a way of assessing attitudes. Too often those being consulted think they are the deciders. This needs to be clear to all.

"We are asking your opinion and preferences. Your wisdom is important to us. We will take all this information and then we will make a decision." Once a decision is made by the committee and *before* any changes take place, everyone is informed (I) of the new times, along with the reasons these were chosen over other alternatives. People are told that this is no longer a time for consultation. The decision has been made. "We are letting you know what changes will happen, when they will go into effect and why this is being done." Such an approach will save much discontent and misunderstanding if used for significant parish decisions.

Another example might be a change in the pastor's living space. For years, the priest's residence was part of the parish office building so that he never really got away from work, except on days off. A house two blocks from the church went on sale. A staff member suggested that this might be a good opportunity for the pastor to finally have some space for himself. "That would be wonderful," the pastor remarked. "But can we afford such an expense just now? It is not in the budget." Who decides this issue?

This raises the question of who is going to decide who the deciders (D) will be. Who decides who decides, in other words? The answer will vary according to the culture and system of each parish. Some would say that the pastor is the one who decides who decides. In the dual-focus system we are suggesting, it might be the pastor and the administrator working in partnership. In other parishes it would be a collaborative effort of the pastoral staff.

Our experience with Catholic parishes suggests another alternative, one in which the pastoral council decides who the D will be: whether they themselves will be the deciders or whether another group or committee will be the deciders. Rather than the council advising the pastor and the pastor making the determination, good pastoring points to a shared ownership by the entire council, a joint effort of council and pastor together. This would be the time for using a consensus style of decision making. The discussion continues until everyone, pastor included, can live with the result. It may not be anyone's first choice, but it is a good solution that council members can own and support.

In the example of a change of residence for the pastor, he brings the matter to the next council meeting and asks them who they think the decider (D) should be. The decision is not to buy the house but whether moving to another location is even an option. After some discussion and much support for the concept of not living "over the store," the council comes to a consensus, with the pastor being an integral and active part of the discussion, that the council as a whole should make this decision. Furthermore, they take the next step and agree that within the next few months a new home should be found for the pastor. Whether or not to buy the house that was up for sale was not the question. That decision the council hands over to the administration commission, instructing them to consult with the finance council about finding the funds for such a move, investigating the house in question about its suitability and consulting often with the pastor about his preferences and desires. The evening finishes with plans about how best to inform (I) the parishioners about the pastor's eventual move out of the rectory and the reasons for the change. Not only does the council decide who should make the decision, it also breaks down the issue into individual decisions, making the first themselves and sending the second one to another group. This is an excellent example of good pastoring on the part of the pastor and council alike.

Balancing Life and Ministry

A fifth essential for good pastoring, along with setting a collaborative tone, leading more than managing, working on a positive image and clarifying the decision making, is finding a healthy balance between parish ministry and one's personal life. Chapter three will deal with this subject at length. It is enough to say here that the more a pastor, or anyone else involved in parish ministry, puts limits on the number of hours he or she works each week, the better the person will be able to listen and respond to people's needs, to direct and work with others, to plan and dream for the future.

Each pastor, each staff person, each pastoral leader has a different pattern for work and leisure, a different measure for what is a reasonable workload. At the same time, parish ministry has a way of capturing people's energies and hooking them into unreasonable expectations placed on them by themselves or others. Good pastoring means finding a life apart from the ministry. Twelve hours a day, six days a week is too much for anyone. It is better to identify what is important and let the rest go or funnel it off to others. No matter how long one works, it will never be enough to meet the demands of the parishioners and the wider community. Heed the advice (mistakenly attributed to Archbishop Oscar Romero) of John Cardinal Dearden in a homily delivered in the Detroit Cathedral on October 25, 1979: "The Reign of God is not only beyond our efforts, it is even beyond our vision. We accomplish in our lifetime only a tiny fraction of the magnificent enterprise that is God's work. . . . Nothing we do is complete, which is another way of saying that the Reign of God always lies beyond us."

Holding Others Accountable

Ronald Heifetz wrote a book called *Leadership Without Easy Answers* in which he describes aspects of leadership that can prove helpful for parishes, especially those operating out of a dual focus of pastoring. One of his contentions is that good leadership means "creating a holding environment for getting others to share responsibility for tough issues, and for protecting voices of dissent."

This is one of the most difficult aspects of pastoring. People do not enjoy being challenged or held accountable, but this is precisely where much pastoring fails. Take St. Timothy's, for instance. It has great potential for good, both among the membership and in the surrounding neighborhood. The staff members are gifted and dedicated people, but they are grossly underpaid. The parish school has a reputation for providing excellent Catholic education, but the faculty is working for less than half the acceptable wage. The parish is struggling for lack of financial resources. The parishioners are not strapped for money; it is just that they have not been challenged to share their financial resources with the parish.

The pastoral administrator, recently hired to work in partnership with the pastor, has as one of her first duties to raise the level of financial contributions. Being new to the parish, she calls together the stewardship committee and inquires about the traditions of asking for money in the parish. She discovers not much has been done. People have been encouraged to acquire a stewardship mentality of giving back to God a portion of the gifts they have received. So far this approach has not translated into higher contribution levels. Parishioners are doing a little better in volunteering their time and talent but not in contributing their financial treasure.

With this information in hand, the administrator makes an appointment to see the pastor. "Joe, you do not have the gift of asking people for money," she says, "nor should you have to do this. That is not what you were ordained to do. This is my task. What I plan to do is call a joint meeting of the finance council, stewardship committee, pastoral council and parish staff to see if we can't come up with a plan. With all that wisdom and experience in one room we should be able to map out a pretty good strategy."

"Sounds good to me," says the pastor. "I'm so happy you are here. I have been trying to do this for years. Good luck!"

Some of the leaders who were invited balked at being part of a "money conference," but with some cajoling and promises of having something to show for their efforts, almost everyone attended. This is one aspect of good pastoring, making demands on people but also providing rewards when people do respond. The meeting created both insightful and realizable results. Within the two-hour time limit, the group settled upon a plan, calling it the "Five Percent Gratitude" plan. The goal was that every registered member of the parish, even the children, would be asked to give five percent of their gross income. The parish itself would lead the way by giving five percent of whatever it received in the collection to needy causes outside the parish.

The approach would be to target individual groups within the parish. The regular contributors would be encouraged to look at the percentage they now give to see if it reached the five percent level and then to make a pledge for the coming year based on that figure. A number of subgroups were identified based on age, place of residence and association with the parish. Some of those targeted were young singles, young married couples, families with teens, older couples whose children had moved away, as well as teenagers and those in grade school.

Each would get a personalized letter explaining the stewardship concept of returning five percent to God for all the gifts received, along with expected contributions for levels of income, a pledge card and a description of the "Five Percent Gratitude" weekend coming up next month. The weekend itself would be a celebration of gifts received. Some people would tell stories of how their giving had brought unexpected blessings, while others would talk about all the good that is being accomplished in the parish through people's generosity.

Throughout this process, the pastoral administrator held those working on the project accountable for whatever they said they would do. The pastor was amazed at all that was being accomplished. Even more, he was amazed by the parishioners' response. A few people grumbled about all this "emphasis on money." Most people, however, got into the spirit of the project, appreciating the spiritual tone of the presentations.

The ritual of people, even children, coming up to the front of church and placing their pledges in the baskets was moving. Some families came up as a unit, the youth group came up as a body, the pastoral council and parish staff members were visible as leadership bodies making their five-percent pledges. Even the pastor put in his card. From that moment on, the financial crisis of the parish tapered off. Salaries for staff and faculty increased, new projects were initiated, needy causes were funded, both in the immediate area and elsewhere around the world. Good pastoring by the administrator, not just the pastor, challenged people to share responsibility for the well-being of the parish. The parishioners' responses exceeded expectations. This is an example of good pastoring as "bearer of the dream and instigator of change."

Holding people accountable is not often encountered in Catholic parishes. Pastor, staff and leaders are afraid to challenge those who do not show up, do not do the job, do not follow through. "We can't do that. They will all leave their ministries. After all, they are just volunteering their time and services." Such an attitude does a disservice to the parish, to fellow workers and to the person or group involved. Someone does not show up to be the lector at Mass. A typical response is to scurry around church to find a substitute and hope one can be found in time. The person who did not show up is never contacted to find out why they were not there. When this happened in one parish, the presider got up and said, "I guess we will have to skip the first two readings. We have no readers." This got people's attention. Two new people volunteered, ones who had never lectored before. They both did a marvelous job. "I did not think I could do that," one woman remarked. "But it is kind of like reading stories to my children. Just make it interesting. I never volunteered before because the ones reading always did such a good job. I was not needed until today."

When vacuums are created, people will respond. In one situation, a member of the liturgy committee called the person who did not show up to read to discover the reason. The person had been called out of town unexpectedly. He had called six others to take his place and found no one, so he just gave up. This was not a good process. Discovering this prompted a new way of operating. Two people volunteered to coordinate the lectors and to arrange backups for emergencies. Holding people accountable resulted in a new and better way of proceeding.

Ronald Heifetz argues that good leadership means "protecting voices of dissent." Along with holding people accountable, this is also an aspect of pastoring that is often forgotten. Who are these "voices of dissent"? They perhaps are the ones who are afraid to speak up at meetings because their ideas may be at odds with the majority or the dominant opinion. The voices of dissent might include those favoring the elimination of the death penalty at a pro-life rally, those pushing for a homeless shelter on parish property, or those seeking a quiet Mass on Sunday morning without hymns and music.

It is the "voices of dissent" that often point the way to a new way of being parish. These are the alienated people on the fringe of the parish who question the accepted way of doing things. They are also the people who, if listened to, can provide new life and vitality to pastoral ministry. The leaders of the Jewish people tried to curtail the actions of Jesus and to dampen the voices of his followers. Yet this is precisely where the Spirit was to be found. Good pastoring keeps an ear out for these voices of dissent and allows them to speak their wisdom, no matter how difficult it is to listen to what they are saying.

Consider the staff meeting in which a decision has to be made about where to go for the annual Christmas party. Ideas fly around the room, one suggestion more elaborate than the next. "We deserve a really nice place this year," one staff person remarks. "We have worked very hard and our budget allows it." A consensus begins to form for dinner at a fancy restaurant. People are getting excited about the prospect. One person, however, remains quiet, not wanting to put a damper on the fun. The pastor notices this and quiets the group so they can listen to Joan's comments. She apologizes for not joining in but feels that she must excuse herself from the party. Everyone is surprised by her response and asks her what the problem is. Her comment is, "Yes, the money is there for the party, and yes, we have worked hard this fall. But I cannot justify the expense when there are so many people, even in our own neighborhood, who are struggling to find toys for their children and food for their Christmas dinner."

That quiets the group and in a more somber mood, they settle on a less expensive place for the party, deciding to add a special contribution to the Giving Tree in the vestibule of the church instead.

Upon reflection the staff was happy for the "dissenting voice" and for the call to simplify. They also enjoyed their fun in dreaming about places they might think of going. The Christmas party turned out to be one of their best celebrations. They also felt good about being able to help others in need. Without the pastor's intervention, this might never have happened.

Pastoring the Pastor

It can happen that a pastor is not well equipped to lead the parish in one or other area. Moreover, it is not likely that a change in the system will take place and someone else will be given the authority to share the pastoring role in order to complement the pastor's shortcomings. What alternatives exist, other than choosing another parish or place of worship? This may be one situation where good pastoring must be assumed by others, either directly or indirectly. Their task is to coach the pastor as to what kind of leadership is required. This is what might be called "managing the politics" in the parish. It will take some thoughtful reflection, a great deal of prayer and rather careful strategizing to accomplish a good result.

Managing the politics means sizing up a particular situation and evaluating what can reasonably be accomplished, given the resources available and the people involved. It means seeking out those who agree with your position and gaining support, as well as connecting with those who oppose your viewpoint to see what common ground exists and what compromises can be reached.

On the parish scene, the first step toward pastoring the pastor is to identify and clearly define the issue or problem. Why is there discontent? Who shares the discontent? What changes can be expected?

Suppose, for example, that the issue is liturgy. The pastor means well but he rambles. The homilies go on too long, have no central focus and do not connect with people's lives. The rest of the Mass is too colloquial and lacks depth and prayerfulness. The pastor makes comments and quips throughout the liturgy, some inappropriate and unnecessary. This makes the weekend Masses go well beyond the one-hour limit. Some people have accepted the situation for what it is, getting whatever they can from the service. Others have given up, either going elsewhere or no longer attending church at all. Still others leave when the hour is up, no matter where this may be in the Mass. The pastor publicly complains about people leaving, not realizing that he is the major cause.

The liturgical director, along with the liturgy committee, is aware of the difficulty but does not know how to confront the issue. The pastor gets defensive whenever the matter is brought up. "There is no rule," he responds, "that the Masses must last only one hour. The Methodists down the street go on for at least two hours and their parking lot is full."

The first step toward confronting this issue is to identify people who have the pastor's ear. These are the people who do not make the pastor nervous, who can approach him in a nonconfrontational manner, persons the pastor respects and takes seriously. Seek out these people. Talk to them about the issue. See if they share your feelings and would be able and willing to speak to the pastor. This will not solve the problem but it can raise awareness. The pastor may not know how he comes across and no one has been able to explain the situation to him in words he can accept and understand.

The next step is to look for an entry point into the pastor's liturgical style. One example is the displeasure he feels about people leaving early. This could be used as a starting point for discussion. Why are people leaving early? Should we ask their opinions? Would any changes in the liturgy change their behavior? Rather than confront the pastor directly, this might open the dialogue about multiple reasons, including the pastor's homilies and style of presiding as one among many. This is one example of "working the process" mentioned in the last chapter.

Another entry point might be the homilies themselves. Bishop Kenneth Untener, who was mentioned at the beginning of this chapter as an example of good pastoring, has all his priests and those who give reflections at Mass go through a homily awareness program. Six people at a time, himself as one of them, tape their homilies and send them around to one another. After listening to the tapes, the group comes together to reflect on the homilies. Also present at the discussion is a theologian, who deals with the content, and an experienced editor, who helps with the style. After spending one session giving one another feedback, the priests go back to their parishes and tape another homily. These too are discussed in the group to see what improvements have been made. As of this writing, every preacher in the Diocese of Saginaw has undergone this process and they are starting up their second round. This process would be a real gift for the pastor mentioned in the example above, as well as for the congregation.

A third strategy in managing the politics of this situation is to support and affirm the pastor in an honest and direct way. Look at what good points he has in his liturgical style. He does connect well with the people. He does greet those coming into Mass and again as they leave. He is friendly and folksy during Mass. It is just that it has no limits or boundaries. He is at ease and relaxed at Mass. This is all to the good. It is just that it can be overdone. One option might be, as affirmation is being given to the pastor, to suggest that when extra rituals are added, such as a baptism or sprinkling rite, that other parts of the liturgy be curtailed. Encourage the pastor to cut back on extra comments or extended prayers during these Masses.

Another strategy to help the pastor is to provide good models of pastoring in the liturgies and in other areas. The way music is announced and led, the way readings and petitions are prepared and presented, the way people are welcomed beforehand and greeted afterwards could become examples of how the liturgy planners would wish the pastor to operate. Other liturgical events, such as communion services, prayer experiences or sacramental preparation could model a spiritual depth and meaning not present at the Masses, all conducted within a reasonable time frame. This will eventually have an effect on the weekend liturgies. As with any system, change one segment and the entire system will be affected.

Besides finding those who can influence the pastor, discovering entry points for change, providing support and affirmation, and modeling good pastoring, a fifth strategy is to establish a structure for easy communication and interaction. In the liturgy this might mean having all the lectors meet together every other month for prayer and reading practice, or arrange for the Eucharistic ministers to gather for a potluck on occasion, or a combined session with all the choirs, old and young alike. This structure allows those who are involved a chance to give feedback and speak their minds. Just bringing them together gets the dialogue going. Invite the pastor to be present at these gatherings so that he might gain insights from the discussion.

First and last, pray. It is a mystery how a given pastor and parish community will operate together and how the pastoring will unfold. Expect the unexpected. The future of this Church, especially on the local level, is not up to us. This is the Spirit's work. Keep an optimistic heart, no matter what the circumstances may be. The conclusion of Cardinal Dearden's homily cited earlier is heartening. "We are workers, not master builders. Ministers not messiahs. We are prophets of a future not our own."

The Covenant of Pastoring

Good pastoring is a call to pastoral partnership. It does not reside in just one person. People pastor one another. They enter into a covenant as God's People. Not only does God hold our hands, as Isaiah 42 suggests, leaders and people grasp one another's hands in this common endeavor. Each person has a part to play, contributing talent and insights, energy and motivation, time and personal resources. The pastor, in partnership with at least one other person, sets the tone of shared responsibility, holding people accountable for what they said they would do. Others do the same for the pastor. This covenant relationship flows in both directions. It involves a mutual give-and-take of leaders and people. Pastoring is not one person but many, working together to be bearers of the dream and instigators of change.

An Example of Good Pastoring
As Manifested by the Leaders and People of
Spirit of Christ Catholic Community, Arvada, Colorado
By
Rev. Robert J. Kinkel, Pastor

As a priest, it is good to look back over your journey and see the hand of God who has shaped and guided all you have done and all that you are becoming. I have had the privilege to serve as an associate pastor in two parishes and am now in my third pastorate. Ordained for thirty years, I have been blessed a great deal and have few regrets. At the present time I am pastor of a large suburban parish with 3,000 families.

In my previous parish assignments, we struggled to find a way to do effective religious education. No matter how many opportunities were provided, there were always some people who felt it inconvenient for their children to attend. What was most exasperating was going to the religious education sessions and asking the students what they remembered from last Sunday's Gospel. Many did not have a clue because they had not attended Mass on the weekend. There was, in my mind, something flawed in our approach when parents brought their children to religious education classes but did not think it important to participate in Eucharist.

When I became pastor at Spirit of Christ parish, I was pleased to see that there was an alternative to handing on the faith to the next generation. Everything related to religious formation is centered around the Eucharist. The gift we offer our people at every Mass on every weekend throughout the entire year is Lectionary Based Catechesis. I have been privileged to be part of this approach for the seven years of my pastorate in this parish.

The parish has moved away from a school classroom approach to an Initiation model. This flowed out of the Rite of Christian Initiation for Adults (RCIA) process. Unlike the classroom model that stresses the transmission of knowledge, textbooks and a systematic organization of beliefs and doctrines, the Initiation model centers on personal commitment, the liturgical calendar, family-centered learning and liturgical rituals. The first approach is more educational and informational, while the latter is more transformational. Our Family Catechetical Director, Maureen DeAoun, supplements the weekly sharing from the lectionary with her own Newsletter. The advantage of this process is that it gives the parents a chance to ask questions in the car on the way home about what the child had experienced. The Newsletter provides a short article on how to connect liturgy and faith to their at-home family experience. This is the best method of family involvement in religious formation that I have experienced and is the reason I believe it be to such a successful aspect of our parish.

The Initiation model follows this process. After the Gathering Song at the start of the weekend liturgies, the children are dismissed from the Assembly. They return at the Preparation of Gifts. The volunteer catechists have all been trained for leading the sessions. They sign up for three-month stints, with the opportunity to renew their commitment each season of the year. There are at least two catechists per session so that the burden does not fall on any one person. Our experience shows that this three-month commitment makes it easier to maintain trained catechists, although some do lead groups for a full twelve-month period.

The parents of children are actively involved in the transformational process. They participate in training sessions at the beginning of the year and are given a parents' book to see what each lesson will contain and what moral, doctrinal and liturgical elements will be included throughout the year. The weekly Newsletter keeps the parents informed and gives them a chance to continue their child's formation in the home.

The parish also offers a sacramental preparation program that is not part of the Lectionary Based Catechesis approach. The parents are the primary educators in this process. The parents come together for adult catechesis in preparation for First Reconciliation and First Eucharist. The sacramental preparation process begins with a simple ritual during the weekend Masses in which the congregation prays for the children and their families as they move toward the celebration of these first sacraments. In this way, the parish as a whole is involved, not just the children and parents.

As a whole, I am most grateful for our Lectionary Based Catechesis and sacramental preparation programs. There are those who complain that their children are not learning anything, and why doesn't the parish offer regular classes for religious education. These complaints are minimal and usually come from those who have not caught the spirit of the parents being the primary educators of their children in the ways of faith. They want someone else to do this for them. Our response is that we, the staff and leaders and catechists, are here to assist and give the parents the means for doing what God has called them to do in their role of parenting, that is, forming their children into Christian adults. This we will not—cannot—do for them.

(Spirit of Christ Catholic Community is located at 7400 W. 80th Avenue, Arvada, Colorado 80003. The phone number is 303-422-9173. Their e-mail address is spirtofCH@aol.com)

CHAPTER THREE

FINDING A BALANCE:
THE EFFECTIVE USE OF TIME

Above all, trust in the slow work of God.
We are, quite naturally, impatient in everything
To reach the end without delay.
We should like to skip the intermediate stages.
We are impatient of being on the way
To something unknown,
Something new.
— TEILHARD DE CHARDIN, SJ

In his book *The Good Enough Catholic, A Guide for the Perplexed*, Paul Wilkes writes that "the notion of being 'good enough' was actually being quite good, and hardly a small achievement in itself." While others might seek perfection, "good enough" and "perplexed" added up for Wilkes "to a way to be formed, and to live, as a Catholic."

"Good enough" is never, however, the accepted practice in a parish. "Perfect" is the more usual rhetoric until the strain becomes too much and something, or someone, "snaps." Council members resign, staffs experience burnout, pastors take sick leaves or retire at an early age (read: before age seventy).

A possible way out of this unending cycle is a change in the system that could have profound effects. Begin by asking what a "good enough" pastor, pastoral administrator, staff person or parish would look like. Consider it a positive and not a negative connotation. The way toward discovering what this would mean is to establish a reasonable workload for those in pastoring and ministerial positions. In a given week, what could people expect from these people? Only those closest to this ministry of leadership have any idea how demanding this job can be, occupying pastor and staff from morning to night—especially night—and for at least six days a week.

The September 25, 1999, issue of *America* contained an article entitled "The 'Good Enough' Pastor." In it I recommended that pastors limit their workload in ministry to fifty hours per week. The response was immediate.

"I read with shock and, quite honestly, some disgust the recommendations . . .," wrote one church minister. She went on to say, "I minister to my family without vacations, sabbaticals or days off. Fifty hours per week is a drop in the bucket" (*America*, October 9, 1999). Others struck a different note. "It takes real effort," wrote a priest, "for all who minister—priests, lay men and women, sisters—to balance how we respond to God's call... 'Enough' is a holy word" (*America*, November 13, 1999). A sensitive chord had been struck. Both priests and people became defensive about the amount of time they spend in their ministry. This issue will not go away as the average age of priests continues to rise and the number of clergy decreases. The temptation is to add more expectations, more duties, more responsibilities to an already full schedule. What is needed is a benchmark for what those in ministry are expected to do with their work time. This could become a common denominator accepted by pastors and people alike. If pastors and staff members choose to do more, putting in longer hours, nothing is preventing them from doing so. But it is no longer *expected* that they do this. If a weekly profile for their jobs could be found, then they would be free to say to others, "I have done what is expected. I can do no more." Others will then have to come forward to pick up the slack and fill the vacuum. This could become a freeing experience, and might even serve as a model to others in ministry and the parishioners themselves.

Such a change could have significant repercussions. For instance, everyone on the staff or in leadership positions, pastor included, would have a clear awareness of how many hours is expected of them each week and how these hours will be utilized for the good of the parish. Concentrating on the pastor would be the place to begin. If this particular benchmark can be established, the rest will more easily fall into place. This is a difficult task, given the history of pastoring. But unless some acceptable measure is found, pastors will be called upon to take responsibility for more and more duties until they are worth little to either themselves or to their ministry.

Establishing a Reasonable Workload

In 1996, a group of priests in Brisbane, Australia, came together to discuss the possibility of relieving the burden on pastors. Most of the priests served multiple parish sites and it was becoming impossible to adequately minister to these various communities. After establishing models for servicing the parishes, the priests turned their attention to their own self-care. One committee drew up a proposal for what might be considered a reasonable workload for pastors and presented it to the gathering of priests. The report created a spirited debate and lively interaction. Some felt that no limits should be placed on what priests were expected to do. Others felt a defined list of tasks would suggest that pastors were shirking their responsibilities. Still others found it refreshing and were encouraged that a reasonable workload could be drawn up as a norm.

With this experience in mind, and the strong response from the *America* article, it seemed a good time to explore what pastors in the United States felt would be a reasonable workload. Accordingly, a number of focus groups for pastors were organized around the country. In preparation for the sessions, the pastors were asked to keep a log of their work-related activities for a given week in order to see how they actually spend their time. Each pastor was to bring another person with them, someone in ministry or in some other helping profession. In this way, we would be able to make comparisons about how both groups, pastors and non-pastors, coped with the demands of their jobs. What we discovered was that the average number of hours per week spent in ministry by the pastors was **sixty-five**. That amounts to about eleven hours per day, six days a week.

Some priests were surprised by the results. One commented, "I had no idea I put in that many hours until I kept track. No wonder I feel washed out at the end of the day." The highest number was eighty-five hours per week. This came from a pastor who said, "I don't take any days off. It comes more in chunks. I'll go for a number of months and then take off for a few weeks to recover." The lowest was thirty-nine hours from a pastor who remarked, "This was not typical for me. I only had two evening meetings that week. Usually I have one or two each night."

In their "sample" week the pastors identified areas where they spent the most and the least time. One pastor remarked, "There is never a typical week. Each one is different. When I start out a day I have no idea what I will have been asked to do when it comes to an end."

Administration and liturgy were the two areas that consumed the most time. Administration included maintenance, correspondence, committee meetings, staff interaction and managing office personnel. Liturgy included presiding at the regularly scheduled Masses, funerals, weddings, reconciliation services, anointings and all the preparation that goes into these services. The *least* time spent by the pastors was involvement in the local community, such as ecumenical associations, neighborhood meetings and community organizing. This was followed closely by professional development. This included reading, updating and personal reflection.

The work hours from those who accompanied the pastors told a different story. These included pastoral staff members, associate pastors, teachers, principals and doctors. In contrast to the sixty-five-hour average among the pastors, the typical partner logged **fifty-three** hours per week. This is just under eleven hours per day, five days a week. Most of the partners had families of their own which put limits on how much time they could spend at work. One partner mentioned, "My struggle is between work and family. It is also between my family and my personal life. I try to find space just for myself, for my prayer, reading and peace of mind. It is a struggle." Most of the partners' time was spent in either administrative duties or in pastoral ministry, such as visiting people, doing interventions and counseling. The partners had difficulty, as did the pastors, in finding time for personal reflection, updating and professional development.

The experience of keeping track of how they spent their workweek was a helpful, although difficult exercise for the participants. As one pastor discovered, "It is not just the ten-minute phone call. It is the twenty minutes after I hang up. It takes awhile to get my thoughts back to what I was working on before the interruption. The needs and concerns of the person on the other end of the line become my own as well. I can't just turn it off and get back to what I was doing."

The purpose of our workshops was not only to uncover how many hours pastors and partners were working. It was to turn their attention to what might be the most *effective* use of their time. Steven Covey in *Seven Habits of Highly Effective People* makes the distinction between what is urgent and what is important in one's workload. We did the same by helping the participants identify issues that are not that urgent but are still important, such as reading, prayer, planning and homily preparation. These are the items that get pushed aside as urgent but less-important issues fill the day. Both pastors and partners worked together to see what changes they could make in order to protect the important issues from getting swallowed up with constant interruptions and less-important distractions. One principal said she was going to try to hold the phone calls for one set period each day so she could be more attentive and responsive to the callers and could still get her work done. A pastor was going to start homily preparation much earlier in the week. "Funny how it happens," he said, "that getting the homily ready can be a nonurgent, important task until Saturday afternoon comes along. Then it suddenly gets to be not only important but *very* urgent as well. Putting it off this way does a disservice to myself and to the parishioners."

One area that used up a portion of the pastors' workweek was the time spent on diocesan projects or pastoral duties not associated with the parish. Pastors serve on diocesan personnel boards, presbyteral councils and marriage tribunals that cut into the time available for parish duties. Some limit, the pastors contended, must be put on these "extra parochial duties" so that they do not become burdensome. Certainly these hours given to extra parochial or diocesan responsibilities should be considered as part of the weekly pastoral workload and not as additional hours beyond those spent in parish ministries.

Steven Covey in his leadership training workshops offers a video that describes the effective use of one's time. A woman is presented with a large bowl of pebbles, the kind used in fish tanks. This was to represent a typical workweek. The pebbles came to within six inches of the top of the bowl. Around the bowl were ten rocks about the size of a fist. Each one of these rocks was to represent an important task or a desired activity for the woman. One she labeled "family," another "exercise," a third "personal reading." Her task was to stick the rocks into her workweek, which was already filled with the pebbles of one's typical time-users. Try as she might, despite digging and pushing and shaking, she could get only five rocks into the bowl before the pebbles started to spill out of the bowl.

The person leading the demonstration then put a new empty bowl, the same size as the first, on the table. The woman was told she could use this empty bowl in whatever way she wished. After sizing up the situation for a few moments, she proceeded to take out the five rocks from the overflowing bowl and to put these, along with the remaining five on the table, into the empty bowl. Once they were all in place, she then poured the pebbles in over the top of the rocks. After shaking and sifting the bowl, she was able to get almost all the pebbles into the new bowl, many more than in the first bowl. The handful she had left over she just threw over her shoulder. "These are not important," she said. "All the important items are already in the bowl."

This story was told to the pastors and the other ministers they brought along with them as a help in determining what would be a more efficient use of their time. Each person was then asked to identify the "rocks" in their lives that they wanted to be sure were included in their workweek. Some of the items mentioned were prayer, reading, spending time with friends and family, hobbies, exercise, journaling, to name but a few. They were then asked to make a commitment for the next six months to incorporate these valued tasks and activities into their daily lives. As a help in this endeavor, each participant was asked once again to pay attention, during a sample week, to how many hours the person spent in ministry. They were also to keep track of how much time each day they made available for their high interest items, that is, their "big rock" activities. To give them support in this effort to redirect their time use, the pastor and person that came with the pastor were to connect with one another at least once a month, either by phone, e-mail or in person, to see how faithful they were to their commitments.

In the fall of 2000, the pastors and partners gathered for a second round of workshops. At this session they were to give a report of how many hours they worked in a given week and whether they made room for desired tasks and cherished interests. The results were gratifying. During the six-month interim, the average number of hours the pastors spent in ministry dropped from sixty-five to **fifty-three**. The partners' work time dropped from fifty-three to **fifty-one** hours per week. This was a significant shift for the pastors and a tribute to their own determination and to the encouragement offered by their mentors.

Some of the areas both pastors and partners were able to protect, despite the pressures of the workload, included visiting friends, priestly support groups, time with family, exercise and liturgical preparation. Still problematic areas, ones that got lost in the hectic pace, included reading, updating, hobbies and staff development. We then asked the participants to make recommendations that could be used as a benchmark for pastors throughout the United States. This is what they suggested:

The pastor should spend no more than fifty contact hours per week doing ministry. In a given week, this would mean that a pastor would be available for meetings, phone calls, liturgies and administrative duties nine hours a day for five and a half days each week. This would serve as the benchmark. Pastors might choose to put in more hours but no more than fifty hours a week would be expected or required.

The question arises whether these fifty contact hours include "on call" time. What about emergencies, people dying in the middle of the night, unexpected tragedies, people showing up at the door after hours? There are two ways to handle these "on call" emergencies. One is to make note of the time these sessions require and then subtract the amount from the fifty hours allowed each week. Another approach is to share the "on call" time with others on the staff or lay leadership so that the pastor is not the only person called outside of business hours. Some parishes have found this to be an effective way of spreading the workload with no detriment to the quality of pastoral care provided. This is another example of replacing the model of parish with the pastor as the *only* center of the circle, to a partnership model with the pastor as one of at least two focal points. The simple task of limiting the number of hours a pastor should be working each week could have the desired effect of fostering a pastoring model in which the pastor shares the workload and the running of the parish with at least one other person. It becomes a dual-focus leadership model.

Establishing a reasonable workload results in spreading out the leadership, showing the need for a dual focus in the parish. Determine how many hours a pastor should be available, keep track of how many hours the person actually spends on the job, and then adjust these hours to fit what might be expected. Those tasks that are left unattended will then have to be either dropped or left for others to manage.

The pastor should have at least one and a half days off each week. The present parish system does not support this. Instead, it encourages pastors to become workaholics. The ideal, in the minds of many parishioners, is to have the pastor always on call, always available whenever they might need a priest. In theory the people affirm regular days off. In practice, if they need a priest, they do not take kindly on being told, "It is his (or in the case of a pastoral administrator, her) day off."

The pastors themselves are ambiguous about getting away. Some consistently disappear for at least a day. They may carry beepers or cell phones for special emergencies, but those who know how to contact them are told to do so only on rare occasions. The pastors involved in our workshops mentioned that a day off was not enough. Having an overnight away from the parish made all the difference. Those pastors who are fortunate to have a home away from home, usually a house or cabin at some distance from the parish, find this a most worthwhile outlet. Others have groups of priests or friends they associate with on their days off, or pursue hobbies and cultural interests that occupy their time away. One essential aspect for establishing a reasonable workload is to have other interests and activities apart from work that call the pastors away and keep them from getting consumed by the ministry.

Although the ideal is to have at least one and a half days a week away from work, the practice, as manifested by many of those pastors attending the focus sessions, showed a different pattern. As one priest acknowledged, "I tried to get away on Mondays, but I found it more and more difficult to do so. After taking care of a few necessary phone calls, and solving an immediate crisis or two, it was usually noon before I was free. So I just spend the afternoon at the gym, read a little and go out to supper with my buddies. This is easier than returning to the office on Tuesday to face a mountain of phone calls and a pile of mail. Now that I have to serve two parishes instead of one, getting away becomes all the more impossible." The other pastors challenged this practice. As one pastor mentioned, "This is not a good precedent to follow. It makes you seem indispensable and creates a poor model for the rest of the staff. Get away. Do yourself and your co-workers a favor."

The reluctance of the pastor to get away for an overnight reveals that the pastor still remains at the center of the circle. Everything depends on his presence and decision making. Efforts to maintain a reasonable workload begin to slip from the pastor's grasp. As a result, many pastors are beginning to resign themselves to one endless cycle of work and pastoral commitments. Various images have been used to describe their situation, such as being pelted to death by popcorn or being at the bottom of a funnel in which everything is being dumped on their heads and they can't escape. All the more reason for a change of system. The funnel should have at least two openings at the bottom, not one. That could reduce the downpour by half if not more.

What about vacations? What would be appropriate? Both the Australian and American pastors suggested four full weeks each year, including four weekends. They also added at least five working days from the parish for an annual retreat. Some said this was not enough. They wanted the option of making an eight-day directed retreat if they so wished. This would mean another weekend away from the parish. The complaint voiced by some parishioners is that the pastor always seems to be "on vacation." The pastor is away in January and again in April, as well as in the summer. Considering the amount of time required for parish liturgies during Christmas and Holy Week, it is not surprising that pastors escape for some free time after these two heavy ministry periods. The benchmark suggested by the pastors and their mentors was four weeks of vacation, which is not an unreasonable concession. If parishioners were made aware of the pastor's plans for vacation and retreat, they would be more understanding and accepting of his time for relaxation and spiritual renewal.

The *Code of Canon Law* supports this time away. Canon 533 states that pastors "may each year be absent on holiday from his parish for a period not exceeding one month, continuous or otherwise. The days which the pastor spends on the annual spiritual retreat are not reckoned in this period of vacation." But who will celebrate the weekend Masses when the pastor is away? Some parishes have the luxury of another priest who can cover for the pastor. This option, however, is becoming less likely as the pool of available priests keeps shrinking. The alternative is to have Communion services on those weekends the pastor is away or to reduce the number of Masses to correspond to the available clergy in the area. The temptation is to make pastors feel guilty about being away and to entice them back early so they can be present at the Masses. This is not a good precedent. The ministry will suffer if the pastor feels caught by parochial duties. Creating a vacuum left by the pastor's absence might uncover new ways of providing communal worship in the parish while the pastor is away being renewed.

We have heard complaints from some pastors that their young associate pastors (priests) are not carrying their load. "When I'm away," one pastor remonstrated, "the associate refuses to do more than three Masses on the weekend. When he is away, I do all five. It is a different breed, these associates." In defense of the younger clergy, we heard one newly ordained speak up, "We will carry our fair share of ministry, but we are not going to devote every waking hour to ministry, and some sleeping hours as well. It is important to maintain boundaries between our personal lives and what we do for a living."

Hard as it may be for some pastors to accept this mind-set, it may point to a direction for future pastors. Ordination is not the equivalent to total absorption in one's work. Putting some distance between work—"what I do"—and personal identity—"who I am"—and discovering healthy boundaries between the two can lead to a more balanced lifestyle, more enjoyable and rewarding ministry and a less controlling, hands-on, style of leading.

The parish offices should not be located in the same place where the pastor lives. In some parishes the pastor lives "over the store," which is not the most conducive arrangement for establishing work limits or creating boundaries between ministry and personal living. This environment dictates total availability, day or night. In other parishes the pastor lives a convenient distance from the church, either at one end of the property opposite the offices or a few blocks away. This little bit of space helps establish a personal life apart from the ministry. The pastor is still reachable for emergencies, but the leaders and people know that when the pastor "goes home," this is time for personal space. This change of location is very helpful in creating a reasonable workload for the pastor. He returns refreshed and with new energy by being separated from work by this short distance. One pastor mentioned that "this little distance makes all the difference. I had no idea that living just a block from the church could have such an influence on improving my disposition."

One source of pressure on a pastor's workload is the rising number of Catholic parishioners to whom each priest is supposed to minister. A research paper presented to the annual gathering of bishops in June 2000 showed that the average size of the Catholic parish increased by sixty-seven percent, from 1,843 in 1950 to 3,086 in the year 2000. Since 1970, however, the total number of priests has declined so that now the majority of parishes are served by only one priest, and over thirteen percent by no resident priest at all. A priest comes from elsewhere to preside at the Eucharist. If no change in the requirements for ordination takes place, this situation will only worsen in the years ahead. In terms of a reasonable workload, what can be expected from the priests?

Pastors should be required to preside at no more than three regularly scheduled Masses on the weekend. On any given weekend, pastors should be expected to preside at no more than two other liturgical celebrations, such as weddings or baptisms. They should be obligated to participate in no more than one reconciliation session per week and no more than one Mass per day during the week. If a funeral is scheduled during the week, then the daily Mass should be dropped or substituted with a prayer service led by another minister.

Liturgical functions are always the most difficult to delineate. It is here that the pastor is most visible and where parishioners' opinions are most vocal when a priest is not available. It becomes even more of a strain when the ordained minister has liturgical obligations outside of the local parish. He may be required to preside at Mass in a mission church or at a neighboring parish that is given direction by a pastoral administrator. This is precisely why some limits need to be placed on what can be expected of any pastor. If the ordained minister has a Mass in another parish, then he can preside at only two in the place where he resides. If he has a wedding elsewhere, then none can be scheduled in the parish. There will always be a cry for exceptions but it is better to seek creative alternatives than demand more time from the pastor. These options might include weddings for more than one couple at a time or wedding ceremonies performed during the regular weekend Masses, or deacons performing wedding ceremonies not involving a Mass and doing baptisms, or other ministers doing the reflections on Scriptures during the Masses in place of a homily by the priest. At one of the follow-up sessions for pastors, a staff member accompanied the pastor. Over the summer this staff person had gotten married. The wedding took place at the regular 5:00 P.M. Mass on Saturday. He found it a wonderful experience and would have had it no other way. "So many more people were able to celebrate with us," he said. "There were plenty of opportunities for our friends and family to toast our union at the reception. But during Mass, the entire community was present to support our marriage."

What people do not realize is the amount of preparation and energy that goes into each liturgical celebration. Part of the number of hours expended each week by the pastor includes large doses of homily preparation, meeting time with couples and parents, filling out documents. The more liturgical celebrations, the more work time devoted to the preparation of these events. As Bishop Untener mentioned in a personal conversation, "It is not the preparation time, it is not the time it takes to drive to and forth to a liturgy. It is a matter of being able to *pray* the liturgy rather than *perform* the prayer. How often in a short space of time can you say from your soul to a new group of people, 'Lift up your hearts'? Most folks can't understand this. They think it is because the priest is too tired. That is not the problem at all."

Changes are being made in a number of dioceses. One pastor mentioned that in his town of four parishes, "we worked out a plan so that there would be no more than three Masses a weekend in each parish and that the Mass schedules would be arranged in such a way that each parish offered Masses at different times. For those who wished an early Mass, this could be found at one of the four parishes. This was true for the other Masses as well. Further, we have a common envelope policy. Parishioners can drop their envelopes at whichever church they visit and their contributions will get back to their home parishes. It is working fine. People are slowly adjusting to the fact that we can't have a plethora of Masses to meet each one's particular schedule."

Bishop James A. Griffin of the Diocese of Columbus, Ohio, wrote a letter to his priests that was cited in the September 15, 2000, issue of the *National Catholic Reporter:* "I believe the time has clearly come to prepare the clergy and faithful alike for a new approach, one which acknowledges that there will be times when, due to a lack of an available priest, there may be no Mass on Sunday in a given place." He went on to say that priests should not be expected to celebrate more than three Masses for Sunday or holy days. The bishop's guidelines urged each parish to have a group of trained persons who would see to the implementation of the parish's own plan for priestless Sundays or holy day celebrations.

Besides establishing a set number of hours per week in the ministry and a clear expectation of days off and vacation time, pastors also need time for professional development. They often complain about having no time to do any reading or for participating in classes on liturgy, Scripture or leadership skills. This opportunity needs to be built into the equation. Not only should pastors have time away for vacation and retreat, they should be given a chance for updating as well. Time spent in these constructive ways will contribute to making pastors happier ministers and more skilled at what they do.

As a result of the pastors limiting their workload, parishes will have to supplement the ministry of the pastor with trained people who will handle upkeep and personnel issues, with pastoral associates who will share the pastor's duties and with empowered pastoral councils and committees to coordinate ministries and share in the decision making. The pastor cannot, should not, do it all. Others, both staff and lay leaders, are ready and willing to pick up the slack. This is a joint venture, pastors and people together.

John F. Murphy wrote a book essay that appeared in the summer 1999 issue of *Church* magazine entitled, "Preparing for a New Pastor." One of the questions he asked in the article was, "What kind of leader do parishes want?" He answered the question by saying that they want a spiritual leader, one who can pastor them rather than be an administrator. In the next breath, however, the people are asking for a pastor "who could point out a vision to them, give them specific objectives to work toward, and then delegate." In all this, he pointed out, "They want an excellent administrator, one who does the work so well that it does not seem to 'preoccupy' one's time but frees the person to do the spiritual pastoring." These two functions of spiritual pastoring and administration, however, do not have to be performed by the same person. Allow the pastor the freedom and the work time to be the spiritual leader. Give over the administration to another person who is a co-leader with the pastor and shares the vision and dream for the parish.

The Benchmarks

Some of the pastors in our focus sessions said it was impossible to arrive at an ideal for their workload. Each person, they said, is so different. The levels of energy, health, stamina and motivation vary widely among priests. Others felt it might be good to offer a criteria to shoot for. "I know some pastors," one pastor remarked, "who could use an ideal as a measure of what is required. From what I have observed, they hardly measure up to the minimum." Thankfully, those who view pastoring more as a job than a ministry, who do not do their fair share and for whom others have to carry the load are the exception. Pastors, staffs and pastoral leaders are, as a whole, a dedicated, prayerful, loyal, altruistic and overworked group of people. They need support, affirmation and relief. As a step in that direction, the following benchmarks or signposts suggest what might be expected of them.

For the number of hours per week, for those involved in pastoral leadership, pastors included, the ideal would be that they work no more than **fifty hours per week**. That would mean working five and a half days a week, nine hours each day. Included in this number is travel time to and from liturgies, appointments and pastoral visits, as well as homily and meeting preparation, background reading and one-on-one interaction.

The priests and those involved in professional ministry should have at least **one and a half days away from pastoral duties every week**. This means creating a heathy distance from work, finding a place where the person cannot be reached except on rare occasions. If the professional minister happens to be a member of the parish, this may require some creative distancing so that the staff person is not approached at the supermarket by a parishioner insisting, "Oh, this will only take a second. Could you tell me . . .?"

Both for priests and pastoral ministers, the benchmark for liturgy is that they would be responsible for **no more than three regularly scheduled Masses per weekend**. The pressure will keep mounting for the priests to take on "just one extra Mass, just for awhile." Then it becomes two and three extra Masses, until the pastor is presiding at five or six a weekend on a regular basis, sometimes driving long distances between sites. Such a person will either collapse from exhaustion or grow bitter and uninspired from this constant routine of Masses. This benchmark serves well for others associated with the weekend liturgies. The person in charge of music or the liturgical coordinator needs relief as much as the pastor. Rather than being present at every Mass every weekend, especially in larger parishes with five or more liturgies each weekend, this benchmark provides an opportunity for others to use their gifts as well. Others can be trained to lead the music, to set up for liturgy, unlock doors or clean up afterwards.

This brings up one essential ingredient of a well-balanced workload. It opens the door for others to assume a greater role in leadership and ministry. Limiting the hours spent by pastor and staff means others will have to take more ownership in the parish. Pastor, staff and parishioners enter into a joint covenant of service to God's People and to the wider community. Ministry does not belong to a few. All are called by baptism to be ministers. Give them the chance to exercise this call by demonstrating a need for their involvement. They must come to recognize that without them, it won't happen. Forego the temptation to rush in and fill the vacuum. In other words, putting in fifty hours a week makes for better pastoring.

Other liturgical benchmarks include **no more than one, and on rare occasions, two other liturgical celebrations per weekend.** This includes weddings and funerals. Adding these extra commitments would amount to four or five Masses for the pastor. This, however, could be reduced by not always having Eucharist as part of the celebration or including it as part of the regularly scheduled liturgies. During the week there would be **no more than one Mass per day per priest**. If a funeral is scheduled, either it is held at the same time as the regular Mass or the daily Mass is dropped. Reconciliation is held to one hour a week or by appointment. Other liturgical celebrations, such as novenas or prayer services, can be led by others or kept to what is reasonably possible, given the fifty hours per week work limit.

Vacations for pastors and professional staff should be set at **four weeks per year, including weekends.** If the professional minister is working a more limited workweek, then the vacation time may not be that long. At the same time, the demands of ministering to people's needs and the drain this causes are not always apparent. What looks like "wasting time with people" can be exhausting. Ministers need adequate time away from work to recoup so they can return to work with fresh energy and resolve.

At least five days each year should be available for retreat, plus five workdays for personal development. Pastors and ministers need time for spiritual renewal and professional updating. Annual retreats are a must, as are days away for updating and workshops. Staff members are better at finding time for this than are the pastors. As a result, priests sometimes feel intimidated by staff members who return to the parish filled with new and innovative ideas. The temptation is to say, "I am too busy to get away." This can sometimes be an excuse for not wanting to give up the controls as the pastor or for being afraid of discovering how "out of date I have become," as one pastor put it.

The focus group participants suggested a sabbatical of at least **four months away from the parish every seven years** for pastors and staff members alike, and this with full pay. The expense to the parish will be paid in full by the knowledge and experience gained by the person on sabbatical. Not only is the person who goes away refreshed, those who remain behind gain as well. One pastor left for a six-month sabbatical shortly after a newly ordained associate pastor arrived. Parishioners were wondering how he would do. "Wonderfully, far better than expected," was the acclamation from staff, leaders and people at the end of the six months. The associate's talent for organization, delegation and teamwork brought new life to the parish. The pastor, in his infrequent contacts with the parish, kept hearing glowing reports about what was going on. It made him wonder about his return and whether he would be welcomed back. It made him study with greater intensity so that he could learn more about his own leadership abilities and discover new ways of operating.

His return was actually a triumph for the entire parish. The associate pastor was grateful to have him back. He had a new awareness and greater admiration for how difficult the job of being pastor can be. "Thank God," he remarked, "I can return to being an associate. When people come to me with a problem I can always say, 'Go see the pastor about that.'" The pastor was happy to be back home and to try out his new skills as a leader. It only took a few weeks and one staff meeting for the staff to realize that a change had taken place. "Let's keep it going," said the pastor. "All that Joe has begun and all that I have learned about pastoring needs to be affirmed and supported. There is no limit to what we can become as a parish community."

Sabbaticals are not only for the pastor. Every staff member needs an extended period away from work to discern, to grow, to try out new experiences. It does a service both to the person on sabbatical and to those who remain behind. Consider the music minister who is away studying new liturgical trends for four months. Someone else must step in to lead the music in her absence. Those already involved, as well as the new recruits who respond to the call for more singers and musicians, take pride in their ministry. Far from the music suffering, it takes on new life because of the determination and gifts of volunteers. The youth minister is given a much needed four-month study tour. The youth council, composed of teens and adults, steps up its efforts and keeps the Sunday evening Mass for teens and the youth program alive and active. When the youth minister returns he wonders whether he should have stayed away longer. Everything is flourishing and many new teens have joined the group. Nothing fosters involvement and ownership more than opening up opportunities and calling people to fill up what is lacking.

Finally, **one's place of work should be separated from one's residence**. The distance does not have to be great, but it should be far enough to make clear the boundary line between ministry and home life. This creates a healthier environment, not only for the pastor or pastoral administrator, but for the staff and parishioners as well.

The following summary, then, is a benchmark for good pastoring:

- Fifty contact hours per week of availability, including diocesan duties
- At least thirty-six hours away from pastoral duties every week
- No more than three regularly scheduled Masses per weekend
- No more than one or two other liturgical celebrations per weekend
- No more than one Mass per weekday, including funerals
- Four weeks of vacation per year, including weekends
- At least five working days away from the parish each year for retreat
- At least five days of professional development per year
- Accommodations separated from the workplace
- A four-month sabbatical every seven years

Confronting the Culture

The effort at establishing a reasonable and effective workload has ramifications far beyond parish ministry. It is an issue facing modern American culture as a whole. A popular book about the Internet, *Lexus and the Olive Tree* by Thomas L. Friedman, describes the drive modern companies and individuals involved in these companies are experiencing to run faster, compete more, produce or die. This leads people to work longer hours and to take work home with them. Through the advances of computers, e-mail, cellular phones, faxes and the Internet, they can remain connected to their work both day and night. The boundaries between work and one's personal and family life are becoming blurred. The obsession to do more, work longer, produce more is summoned up in the slogan "24-7." That translates into the drive to work twenty-four hours a day, seven days a week, which flies in the face of all we have been advocating in this chapter about finding a balance in one's use of work time.

The question remains: Will this cultural drive to work harder and longer hours be confronted by the local parish, or will parishioners see the same hectic pace played out by their spiritual leaders as they do in other areas of their lives? The answer to this question begins with the pastor and staff taking a careful look at how they spend their own time. They need to make commitments to curtail their hours in order to stay within the bounds of a reasonable workload. The benchmarks enunciated in the previous section are helps in this direction.

Once the pastor and staff commit themselves to a reasonable workload, they need a mentor to hold them accountable to their commitments. Pastoral ministry is a deceptive and jealous mistress. It keeps making demands and confronts the ministers with guilt feelings for not being available or on call well beyond what is required. A mentor helps keep the ministry in balance. For most people in need it does not matter who fulfills that need, so long as it is taken care of. "My father is dying. Come to the bedside." They think a priest is the only solution. Once they discover, however, a sensitive, caring pastoral-care minister, their needs are addressed. "What are the requirements for my son's confirmation?" They think only the youth minister can answer their question. They are surprised to learn that a volunteer on the confirmation team can do just as well. The need is met. A mentor can help the pastor and staff members sort out these issues and the feelings that go with them. The mentor does not have to be a psychologist, counselor or spiritual director. Pastor and staff can mentor one another. All that is needed is someone who can listen well and give honest feedback and insights. People need to be encouraged to share in this open atmosphere of mutual ministry.

Associated with establishing a reasonable workload is the realization that the ministry and the pastoring can continue, even flourish, without the pastor or staff person having to be always present or in charge. This can be a humbling realization. If followed to its logical conclusion, it would mean letting go of the controls, of the need to be the primary decision maker and the one to whom people turn when in crisis or in need. Pastoring becomes a joint effort. This takes some getting use to, a great deal of practice, and experiences of both success and failure in the effort. In the long run, it leads to a better parish, one in which pastoring is a call to partnership and ministry, a covenant relationship between the leadership and the baptized.

This is an ongoing struggle, one only obliquely realized. But the attempt is worth the effort because it is such a brilliant example to the parish community. "Simplify your lives. Don't push so hard to produce and keep up the pace. It will only lead to failure. Enjoy life. Separate work and home life. Love each other. Find some quiet time and pay attention to inner longings and desires. It is the God within who is speaking to you. Be gentle, be generous, be a blessing, be at peace. Find time for a Sabbath day while you have the energy and health to enjoy it. Work hard but work smart. Do not let it consume you and all you hold dear."

Words, however, will never convince people. Actions will. Having a concrete model to look to as an example of a reasonable workload and staying within realistic boundaries is what gets people's attention. That is why finding a balance is so important for pastors and staffs and parish workers. The implications of this go well beyond the individual and group; it changes the culture of the parish and those who belong to it.

But people do need words as well. They need to be told what a typical workweek for the pastor and staff looks like, how they struggle to find a balance and what implications this has for others who share the load. Most people feel the pastor presides at liturgy and makes a few pastoral visits. That is the extent of the workload. How little they realize what is really involved. The same is true for the religious education director, the youth minister, the pastoral associate, the administrator. One pastor asked the people during the weekend liturgies to put down how much time they thought he spent in each aspect of ministry, ranging from homily preparation to phone calling, from hospital visits to the time spent in travel. When he asked them to total up the hours, people were surprised that for many it amounted to over ninety hours a week. Then he told them what his typical week looked like and how he had been working at reducing his hours, allowing others to assume greater responsibility in running the parish. The general response from the congregation was twofold. First they had no idea how he did spend his time. Second, they congratulated him for his efforts and pledged their support and cooperation. His response was, "I wonder why I didn't think of doing this a long time ago."

A Message to the Bishops

The final item on the agenda of the follow-up sessions for pastors and mentors was what they felt should be said to the bishops about their workload. Some of the suggestions are as follows:

Pay attention to the workload you are expecting of pastors, lest you continue to lose the few you have. Workaholism is not a gift of the Spirit. Pay attention to this in your own life as well.

Support your priests and pastoral ministers. Stand strong as a national body, even if it means coming in conflict with higher authority.

Recognize the people's right to the celebration of the Eucharist. Provide a forum in which the parish community can call people to priesthood, even without the requirement of celibacy. Also recognize the movement of the Spirit in the evolution of the ministry of women in the Church today.

Many priests are living an emotionally and spiritually unhealthy lifestyle at the present moment. Both priests and parishioners are suffering because of this. There needs to be practical limits placed on the number of Masses priests are required to celebrate.

We are not the enemy. We love the Church just as you do. Please think of us that way. Listen to the people and be closer to them. Encourage sabbaticals, study opportunities, retreats and spiritual development for the priests, staffs and pastoral ministers.

Seriously look at and really *own* the consequences of not dealing with the issues related to ordination, such as burn out among priests, their physical and mental health being compromised, less time for meaningful ministry, people being deprived of Eucharist and sacraments. Recognize the need for priests to have a life of their own.

Identify the ideal workload for pastors and promote it throughout the diocese. Push for the celebration of weddings during the regularly scheduled weekend liturgies. Advocate for the ordination of married men.

Put as much time and effort into making sure priests take time for retreats, personal updating and recreation as is given to the Annual Appeal throughout the diocese. Provide as much funding for the development of lay ministry and staff development as is given to the formation and preparation of future priests.

Entrust the administration of the parish to someone other than the pastor. When appointing pastors, consider appointing a team along with the new pastor that would include qualified lay people to share in the running of the parish.

Encourage priests to live in communal settings with other priests who might serve a number of different parishes, but in a place removed from any one of the parishes. Also, foster more dialogue and sharing with other denominations to see how they cope with the pressures of pastoral ministry and in this way, learn from one another.

Finally, one added this message to the bishops: "One of your own, the late Joseph Cardinal Bernardin, wrote to his priests before he died, 'Get away from the paperwork. Ask yourself, When people come to church, are they finding Jesus? If they are not, then they are wasting their time. People simply want us to be with them in the joys and sorrows of their lives. In light of that, priests need to be the face of Jesus to people. They need to have time to do this and to get away from paperwork. Compassion comes before compliance.'"

A Covenant with Oneself

A change of attitude and practice toward an effective workload is already taking place. One example of this is the shift in the pastors' use of time from the first focus session to the follow-up six months later. They made good choices about how best to use their limited work time. They made a commitment to concentrate on tasks that were important to accomplish, not just urgent and pressing. They formed a personal covenant to let go and allow others to share their ministry. As a result, pastoral staffs and parish ministers are taking initiative and are assuming greater ownership in the running of the parish. One hopeful insight amid these efforts is the conclusion to the quotation from Teilhard de Chardin, SJ, that began this chapter. Once we incorporate this into our work ethic, it will free us from compulsion and provide us with the gift of serenity amidst the unending demands of ministry.

> Only God can say what this new spirit
> Gradually forming within you will be.
> Give our Lord the benefit of believing
> That God's hand is leading you,
> And accept the anxiety
> of feeling yourself
> in suspense
> And incomplete.
>
> — Teilhard de Chardin, SJ

Ps 127

CHAPTER FOUR

A FRAMEWORK FOR PLANNING: BOTH LINEAR AND CIRCULAR

Jethro said to Moses, "What are you doing for all these people?
Why do you sit alone with all of them standing around you
from morning till evening?"
"The people come to me," Moses answered,
"to seek God's guidance" . . .
But his father-in-law said to Moses,
"This is not the best way to do it."
— EXODUS 18:14–17

What Jethro goes on to explain to Moses is a new way of operating. He suggests that Moses find wise, capable, God-fearing leaders and appoint them "over units of a thousand, of a hundred, of fifty or of ten." He goes on to say, "In this way your burdens will be lightened, and they will share it with you. If you do this, God will give you strength and you will be able to go on." What Jethro was offering to Moses was a structure that would, in his words, "regain peace and harmony" (cf. Exodus 19).

In the same way, in seeking to establish a covenant between God and the people, a modern parish must have a structure or framework out of which to operate and assure a productive future. What is described in this chapter are various approaches to structure as a means for including more than just a few insiders in making plans for the future. These are possible models. There are many others.

Whatever the structure, it is only as good as what it allows the leaders and the people to realize as a parish community.

Ingredients of a Structure

In working with parish leaders, we occasionally ask them to draw a picture of their current parish structure. This is not what it is *supposed* to look like on paper or in the bylaws but a depiction of how it *actually* is operating. The results are often humorous and very revealing. Representatives from the same parish will draw completely different diagrams depending on each person's perception and experience of the parish. In some descriptions, the pastor may play the dominant role, located at the center of the structure. In others, the school may take center stage, or the choir, or the women's club or a ministry of one or other staff persons. The purpose of this exercise is to show that the structure that is intended is not always the one that is operative. It also provides an invitation to the pastor, staff and leaders to discuss the ingredients that should be present in any structure that will help the parish function "in peace and harmony."

However a parish is structured, one ingredient it should foster is **clear and direct lines of communication.** Does the way it is organized keep people in touch with one another? The best way to do this is to create a "geography of communication." This means setting up an environment in which people have to bump into one another, are at least occasionally in the same room with each other, have a regular routine and set time for interaction.

When staffs complain about a lack of communication, it is helpful to look at where the offices are situated. If there is a physical separation of staff members, some in the parish office and others scattered elsewhere, this makes communicating difficult. To overcome this separation they must set up a regular schedule of interaction, such as sharing e-mail every morning before they start their day, or coming together for meals and breaks to report on activities. One model for parish organization puts all the key leaders together in the same room at least once a month. Without this common geography people tend to go about their own business not knowing what others are doing.

A second ingredient of a well-functioning structure is one that **spreads out the visioning and decision making**. The story of Moses in

Exodus identifies him as the one to whom everyone came with complaints and problems. Jethro's reaction was that "you will only wear yourself out and wear out all the people who are here. The task is too heavy for you; you cannot do it by yourself." A more successful structure utilizes the insights and talents of as many people as possible. This approach, of course, has its liabilities. It creates a tension between individual ideas and visions—"*I* think this is what we should do"—and the ideas of the group as a whole—"*We* think this is the best plan." This is a healthy tension. It keeps the dialogue creative and the options fresh. A good structure must not only allow but encourage this "I-We" tension. It must also, however, be facilitated by a leader who maintains a common direction for the group while not stifling individual initiative.

The structure is not an end in itself. It flows out of the group's **core values and underlying mission**. If outreach to the poor and marginalized is an agreed upon value, then the structure must make this possible. If lifelong learning is part of the group's mission, then the structure must help foster this. Because structure and values are so closely connected, it is possible to discover a group's dominant values by studying its operating structure. Some of the pictures people drew of their parish structure, for instance, revealed that shared decision making is not a core value for the parish leadership, no matter how insistent the rhetoric that this is part of its mission as a parish community.

Any effective structure must have built into it the means for **holding people and groups accountable** for what they said they would do. One example of a structure for lectors and Eucharistic ministers includes a monthly schedule sent out to all those involved in these ministries. For those who can't meet their obligation, they are to find their own substitutes. Everyone receives a complete list of names and phone numbers to contact. On paper it looks like an excellent structure. In reality it is falling apart. Why? Because no one holds the volunteers accountable for getting replacements. A more workable method is to appoint overseers, as Jethro suggested to Moses, who make sure that if people fail to show up or to get a replacement, they are contacted to discover why and what changes need to be made in the future. It shows the volunteers that their obligations are taken seriously.

Another ingredient of a well-functioning structure is to **keep the boundaries open**, allowing, even encouraging people to move in and out of ministry frequently and easily. In such a structure, there is a regular turn-over of membership, with established limits of involvement. A structure that allows people to remain in one position for too long a period is susceptible to a staid routine and the establishment of cliques and in-groups. If, on the other hand, people know there is a set tenure for involvement, this fosters interest and creativity, and lessens the occasion of burnout and boredom.

Finally, whatever the structure, it should provide **automatic links and connections** between groups and ministries. Bridges are built and gaps are filled in so that people are in touch with the scope and responsibilities not only of their own activities but of those in other groups as well. This helps reduce overlap and duplication and helps groups remain complementary to one another. It also lessens the occasion for conflicts and ill feelings between them. One way of providing these inter-group connections is to have individuals belonging to or present at more than one group or func-tion at a time. Nothing provides better linkage than having a person pres-ent who has direct experience of the other group or ministry.

In summary, the checklist for a viable parish structure is as follows: It should be one that:

- Fosters clear and direct communication
- Spreads out the visioning and decision making
- Flows out of the group's mission and core values
- Holds people accountable
- Keeps boundaries open and has limited tenure
- Provides linkage between groups and individuals

Parish Coordinating Groups

A number of parishes across the country, both large and small, have utilized a structure that manifests the ingredients listed above. Some of the advantages of this structure is that it helps eliminate extra meetings, pro-vides instant and direct communication among groups, increases parish-ioner involvement and provides a direction and vision for all aspects of the parish. Here is how it works.

The first step is to establish coordinating, visioning, leadership groups in five areas of parish life. This is not a new concept. Many parishes have such groups. In some places they are called *commissions*, in other places, *committees* or *ministry groups*. Whatever the designation, they operate as mini-councils, giving direction to a particular aspect of parish ministry. In the area of worship, for instance, six to ten people, all of whom are involved in some aspect of the parish liturgies or other prayer experiences of the parish, make up one such group. They come together to reflect on what is happening, what is going well, what is missing and what more could be done. Just as the pastoral council sets the direction for the parish as a whole, so does this group do it for worship and spiritual life.

This group is not the liturgy planning committee whose task it is to plan the liturgies for each season of the year. If, however, the liturgies are not being planned well, it would be the worship coordinating group that would either hold the committee accountable or, if no such group existed, see to it that one is formed. This worship coordinating group would also dream about all that the weekend liturgies could be, from music to hospitality, from homilies to congregational participation. Each year this worship coordinating group would construct one or two goals for the area of worship and spirituality, as well as establishing action steps to reach these goals. It would also see to it that all aspects of the liturgy and prayer experiences are well coordinated and that all are working toward a common end and in the same direction.

Other visioning, coordinating groups include those working in community building, education and formation, outreach and evangelization, administration and finance. The community-building group, for instance, would help foster a welcoming, communal spirit in the parish. One of its goals might be to sponsor a parish social or fun event for each month. This creates a regular tradition of social gatherings throughout the year. These social events might include a picnic in July, a back-to-school party in August, a ministry fair after the Masses one weekend in September, an October Fest, a Thanksgiving dance and a Christmas party, to name but a few. Not only does the community-building group set up a regular schedule of events, it also establishes separate committees to coordinate each event. This will be discussed more at length in chapter six.

The education and formation coordinating group has as its task a common direction for all areas of religious formation. It might foster not only a Catholic School's week in January, but a Religious Formation week that shows off all that the parish is doing to help further people's understanding of their faith, both old and young. This coordinating group would also look at how to bridge the gaps from one age level to the next. They would see to it that significant events are planned to ease the transition from grammar school to high school, from senior year to college. Special attempts would be made to remain connected with those away at school, and to provide events for young adults, both single and married. Not that the formation coordinating group would do all this but it would encourage others involved in religious education to help people through these important transitions.

The area of outreach covers a variety of ministries, including pastoral care to the sick and homebound, addressing social needs and areas of injustice, connecting with the inactive and those on the fringes of the parish and society. A number of parish committees and individuals usually handle this area. What is needed is a coordinating group that establishes links between these groups, keeps their work present before the parish community, sets a unified direction for pastoral outreach in the parish and uncovers areas of need not dealt with by existing ministries.

Administration is the fifth area given direction by a visioning, coordinating group. Each Catholic parish is required to have a finance council. This is one aspect of administration. Others include buildings and grounds, communications and publicity, fund-raising and stewardship of treasure, personnel and volunteer coordination. This administration coordinating group might decide to concentrate on communication as its goal. It might create a publicity committee that specializes in getting the word out about parish events, either through newsletters, posters, banners or e-mail. Or the coordinating group might focus on plant expansion, arranging for a long-range plan for parish buildings that will meet present and future needs.

As with the other coordinating groups, representatives from various aspects of administration make up the group. Depending on the size of the parish, there would also be a staff resource for each coordinating group. The staff person would not run the group but would provide background, insight and professional expertise as needed.

Members of the coordinating groups would discern among themselves who will be the chairperson. Some parishes have introduced the option of having two people take the position as co-chairs. In this way, not one person, but two lead the group. They work together as partners, taking turns running the meetings. The co-chairs and the staff resource person make up the agenda for the meeting beforehand. They then initiate a phone chain of the membership, each calling one person, who calls the next person on the list, and so forth, until all are contacted. The purpose of the calls is to remind the members about the next meeting and to fill them in about the agenda so people can come prepared for the meeting.

Once a year, all the people who are involved in one or more ministries and organizations of the parish gather together for a common meeting lasting no more than two hours. This is called a Gathering of Ministers. The purpose of this assembly of ministers and volunteers is to assess what has happened over the year in each area of the parish, to suggest directions for the coming year and to determine who should be the new members of the five coordinating groups.

Suppose this Gathering of Ministers takes place following the noon Mass on a Sunday during Lent. A few hundred people show up at 1:00 P.M. in the gym. They drop off whatever snacks they have brought and move out to the gym for common prayer together. After an explanation of the day and a ten-minute communal prayer, people are asked to divide into five different areas depending on each person's ministry or involvement. Those who are associated with more than one area must choose which aspect will be their primary focus for the coming year. For instance, someone who is a lector, a visitor to the sick and a classroom aide can still do these ministries, but the person decides that the main focus for the coming year will be pastoral care instead of liturgy or formation. So the person heads off to the "outreach" section. The intention is to help people maintain a balance in the number of parish commitments they make, as well as opening up positions for others to fill. One implication of the person choosing outreach as the focus for the coming year is that he or she may not read at Mass as often as in the current year. This opens up this ministry to new people and brings in fresh blood to that area.

Participants spend time discussing what were significant events over the course of the year in each of the five areas. For example, the worship ministers might reflect on Christmas and Easter liturgies as high points, as well as the recent parish mission, the special prayer events held in church or the introduction of weekly adoration last fall. The visioning, coordinating group leads the people through an evaluation of what has been accomplished, describes the goals it is now working on for the coming year and seeks ideas of what might be new initiatives for the future. The gathered ministers are also aware that this is the time that a third of the coordinating group will have completed their three-year commitment of coordination and leadership. Names are surfaced from the gathering about who the new members might be. These names are given to members of the coordinating group. All the nominees are then invited to a special discernment meeting taking place the next month.

After an hour, all five sub-gatherings are invited back to the gym for reports and celebration. The Gathering of Ministers meeting concludes at 3:00 P.M., each person having a better sense of what has happened and what will happen in at least one area of parish ministry. The coordinating groups have also obtained the names of candidates who said they would be willing to fill the vacancies left by those terminating their term on the coordinating groups.

A Common Leadership Night

With the coordinating groups in place and the process established for adding new members to the groups through the Gathering of Ministers, the next step is to add the one ingredient that brings it all together.

One night each month all the visioning, coordinating groups meet for prayer, deliberation, reporting and socializing. Thirty-five to forty people gather for prayer at 7:00 P.M. One of the coordinating groups leads the ten minute prayer. The groups share this task on a rotating basis. Following prayer, the pastor or one of the staff members gives a five-minute instruction on some aspect of leading or visioning as a help to all those present. At 7:20 P.M., the five coordinating groups head off to separate rooms to work on their own agenda items. Following the Gathering of Ministers, for instance, one task might be to include all those nominated to be members of the group for the coming year. Time would be spent in a discernment process to determine who will succeed those going off the coordinating group. At other times, agenda items might include evaluation of groups and ministries associated with that coordinating group, selecting one or two goals for the coming year or setting up committees and sub-groups to accomplish the goals.

At 8:20 P.M., all five groups reassemble to give two-minute reports about what they have been discussing or seeking to accomplish. A gentle but firm timekeeper makes sure that each report does not go over the two-minute limit. At 8:30 P.M., everyone breaks for socializing. The treats are provided by one of the coordinating groups, again on a rotating basis. At 8:40 P.M., the members of the pastoral council withdraw for their own meeting. Everyone else is free to leave, to remain in order to enjoy one another's company or to sit in on the pastoral council meeting.

The pastoral council can get right to business without having to listen to reports. That was already done in the larger gathering. This structure works best if the council is made up of representatives from each of the five coordinating groups, two from each one. The advantage is that membership in the coordinating groups gives people a chance to learn how the system works and what the task of visioning and coordinating is all about. It also furthers close communication between all aspects of parish ministry because each person is directly involved in one of the visioning, coordinating groups.

Another help toward better communication is the written report, no longer than one paragraph, that representatives from each coordinating group bring to the council meeting. These brief reports are added to the council minutes and are published as an insert to the bulletin each month for all to see. The total membership of the pastoral council includes two people from each coordinating group, the pastor and one staff representative selected each year by the staff. This staff person assures a close connection between staff and council, freeing the pastor from this added task. This is another example of a dual-focus approach to parish leadership. The business of the council is concluded at 9:30 P.M., all returning home with a sense of accomplishment as the leaders of the parish community.

The schedule for the evening looks like this:

7:00	Common Prayer
	Each coordinating group takes a turn leading prayer
	A short instruction on some aspect of leadership and planning
7:20	Break into coordinating groups to work on their agenda items
8:20	Group Reports followed by Socializing
	Limit reports to two minutes per group
	One person is appointed to keep track of time and limit the reports
	Each coordinating group takes a turn providing refreshments
	Each group hands in a brief written summary after its report
8:40	Pastoral Council meets to work on its agenda items
	No reports needed from the coordinating groups, only clarifications

9:30   Pastoral Council Adjourns
            Pastoral Council Minutes and Group Reports are published in
            the parish bulletin or newsletter

As claimed at the outset, this structure accomplishes many things. First, it eliminates extra meetings. Parishioners have an easier time volunteering for leadership positions if they know it will not drag them into a multitude of meetings. If they know that all that will be required is one meeting each month that is well run, stays within limits and has something to show for one's efforts, they are much more likely to offer their services. Some parishes have made adaptations to this structure, having a common leadership night every other month, which allows groups to hold individual meetings on their own in between. This, however, still amounts to only one leadership meeting per month.

A second advantage to this structure is that it provides instant and direct communication. One great help to better communication is to get everyone in the same room and give them the chance to report to one another about what they are doing. The timekeeper is of critical importance. Nothing kills a meeting quicker than to have one person dominate the reporting for an extended period of time.

This structure increases involvement, especially by spreading out the leadership, visioning and decision making. This encourages greater ownership and interest, leading to higher involvement. One help in this direction is the annual Gathering of Ministers which opens up new avenues and positions for participation in parish ministries. There is no better way to get people to volunteer than to demonstrate a real need for their involvement.

Finally, this structure provides direction for all aspects of parish life. The staff may be able to do this on its own, but then the parish becomes staff driven and is an entity "owned" by the staff. The pastoral council can be given this task, but a modern parish is so complex and multi-dimensional, it needs more than one group to give it direction. The five visioning, coordinating groups provide this service. They set the direction in each area of ministry, leaving the council free to give direction to the parish as a whole.

There is no one way to structure a Catholic parish. Each place has its own culture and characteristics. What is offered here is a general floor plan that can be adapted and adjusted to meet particular needs and desires. The outline, however, remains the same. Spread out the visioning and owner-ship by creating groups in each area of parish ministry. Gather together all those involved in ministries and organizations on a yearly basis in order to assess past and future directions and to add members to the visioning, coordinating groups. Have all the coordinating groups meet on the same night and at the same time. This means that people cannot serve as mem-bers of more than one group at a time, leaving room for more people to become involved. Finally, create the pastoral council out of the coordinat-ing groups in order to have trained people on the council and to maintain close communication. Continually recruit new people into parish min-istries and organizations as a pathway into parish leadership. A viable parish structure must provide the occasion and opportunity for as many people as possible to realize their potential as ministers, leaders and visionaries for at least one aspect of parish life.

A Yearly Tradition of Planning

The structure described above works best if there is a predictable pat-tern of implementation that is repeated each year. The tradition begins in late August with a review by all parish groups and ministries for the coming year. This is the first step toward making up job descriptions for each ministry. For example, in seeking Communion ministers, what is required of a person who brings Communion to the sick and homebound? How many hours each month will this involve and what time of the day or day of the week should it be done? How many people will need to be visited by this one person? What training will be required? Will the vol-unteer be expected to attend any meetings during the month? What skills are needed?

Each volunteer position should have a one-page summary of what the job entails and what will be required of the person, both in time, prepara-tion and skill. With these job descriptions in hand, the council, staff and coordinating groups sponsor a Parish Ministry Fair sometime during September. This is a gala affair held on Saturday and Sunday following each of the Masses. The gathering space, gym or parish center is prepared with booths displaying all the various ministries, organizations and activities operating in the parish. Parishioners are encouraged to pick up display materials and description cards for each area of involvement. Some parishes even change the location of the Masses from the church to the gym or under a tent for that weekend in order to capture people's attention and to highlight the ministries. Whatever the location, special refreshments are included as a way of drawing people to the booths. In one parish the smell of popcorn greeted people as they came out of church enticing them into the Ministry Fair area.

A week or two after the Ministry Fair is the time people are asked to share their gifts of time, talent and treasure for the coming year. They choose a ministry for volunteering their time and pledge a percentage of their income, bringing their commitment cards to the front of the church during each one of the weekend liturgies. The coordinating groups split the commitments of time and talent, making sure that those who volunteered are contacted within a two-week time frame. Nothing discourages involvement so much as volunteering for a ministry and never being contacted or invited to participate.

People fulfill their commitments throughout the year, receiving training as needed and taking part in sharing groups of those involved in similar ministries. All are given frequent affirmation and support for their generosity. The coordinating groups continue to meet on a regular basis, coming together on their common Leadership Nights each month.

In March, the pastoral council and coordinating groups sponsor the Gathering of Ministers. This is the time, as mentioned earlier, where all those involved in groups and ministries have a chance to look at what has happened so far this year and to begin making choices about continuing in their present area of ministry or choosing another for the coming year. This is also the time people are selected for leadership positions on the coordinating groups and eventually on the pastoral council. At the April Leadership Night, new recruits are discerned for membership on the coordinating groups. Those who have fulfilled their term of office sit down with the new people and explain "how we do things around here."

This special training session for new members is a key ingredient of this structure. All those who are going off the coordinating groups and all the new members come together for a two-hour meeting. The veteran members each have a copy of the parish leadership manual. Some parishes have called this their "Covenant Booklet" because it articulates the areas of commitment and agreement that all those serving on the staff, council and coordinating groups make to one another. The booklet contains a compilation of all that is needed for those in leadership positions in the parish.

This includes a diagram of the parish structure, a description of each coordinating group and the ministries and groups associated with each of the five areas. It also contains the names and phone numbers of current members, goals and action steps for the coming year, a list of planning events that take place each year, such as the Ministry Fair and Gathering of Ministers, as well as explanations of how decisions are made and what group or staff person is responsible for each aspect of parish ministry.

After an initial gathering of the whole group for introduction and prayer, people break into pairs, one person leaving the coordinating group with one person coming on. During this one-on-one interaction, the veteran member goes through the Covenant Booklet with the new person, handing it over to that person as a sign of passing on the authority to the new guard. (See *Transforming the Parish*, Forster and Sweetser, pp. 85–86 for an explanation of what is contained in the Covenant Booklet.)

Those who have participated in this training session have been grateful for the experience. For those leaving the groups it has been a time for putting closure to their leadership position and a celebration of all that was accomplished during their term. For the new members, it has been an excellent way to "get up to speed" at the start of their leadership commitment. Because all those on the pastoral council also serve on one of the coordinating groups, there is no need to have a separate training session for council members. They are able to learn "on the job" because they have already had experience in parish leadership by serving on one of the coordinating groups. Many parishes using this structural model have a three year term for the coordinating groups and a two-year term for the pastoral council. That way, a person who has completed one year on a coordinating group would be a likely candidate for serving on the pastoral council. Each year, one third of the coordinating groups leave and are replaced by new members nominated during the Gathering of Ministers. Once the new coordinating membership is set, one person is discerned by the group to serve for the next two years on the pastoral council, while still maintaining membership on the coordinating group. This way, half of the pastoral council changes membership each year.

During the May Leadership Night, all the new and current members, as well as those leaving the coordinating groups, participate in an evaluation session. They identify what worked in each area of ministry and what didn't work. They also investigate the *reasons* things worked or didn't work so as not to repeat the same mistakes next year. If having "home-made treats" helped make the Ministry Fair more successful this year, then do it again, not only for next year's fair, but for other events as well. If charging for coffee and donuts after the Masses didn't work, make it free next year and build the expense into the budget. If Monday night is not a good evening for the Leadership Nights because of football, try out another night during the fall season and see how it turns out. The May Leadership Night is also the time that each coordinating group discerns who of their number will serve on the pastoral council for the next two years.

The June Leadership Night is for setting goals for each aspect of the parish. Based on the evaluations from the previous month, this is when the coordinating groups decide their focus for the coming year, while the pastoral council maps out the direction for the parish as a whole or establishes a common theme for the coordinating groups to incorporate into their goals and action plans.

The rhythm of the year includes not only planning but socializing among the leaders, as well as prayer and retreat time together. Some parishes, instead of having a May or June Leadership Night, decide to have an overnight away from the parish for prayer, evaluation, goal setting and having fun together. Whatever the method, the rhythm of the year is as follows:

July Aug. Sept. Oct. Nov. Dec. Jan. Feb. Mar. Apr. May June
—Ministry Job Descriptions—Ministry Fair—Commitments—Gathering of Min.—Evaluations—Goals—

Making Plans

Setting up an effective structure is only part of the framework for parish planning. How the structure is utilized for creating a plan of action is critically important if the parish is going to move to a new level or remain, instead, on a plateau with little movement toward a new future. For instance, St. Mary's was a parish with good intentions but little to show for its efforts at goal setting and planning. It had all the talents and expertise it needed, located among its own membership. Despite this resource, it was not able to develop a plan on its own. The pastor, staff and leaders decided to investigate what other resources were available, both in the local area, in the diocese and in other parts of the country. Eventually they chose a resource that best fit their needs and began the formal process of formulating a strategic plan for the future of the parish.

The process St. Mary's chose had three parts. The first step was to "ask the folks." Through the use of a random-sample survey, they gathered as much information about the current state of the parish as possible. The leaders were amazed at how much the parishioners were willing to share their attitudes and opinions once given the chance. The survey uncovered reactions toward the liturgies, community life, educational programs, outreach ministries, pastoral care and administration. The leaders also did some reflecting about the parish, including such issues as what was the unique character of each of the weekend Masses, how volunteers were matched to the tasks that fit their capabilities and desires, what options for religious formation were possible besides the formal religious education programs that currently existed in the parish.

Each of the coordinating groups and areas of ministry had its own set of questions to answer. This information-gathering exercise not only provided valuable information about the current state of the parish, it also raised interest in the planning process itself. The second step toward forming a plan was to schedule a few weeks for strategic planning that would concentrate the efforts of the entire parish and help focus people's attention on future directions. This two-week period provided St. Mary's with the opportunity to step out of its current situation and reflect on what *could be* with fresh ideas and new energy.

The parish hired outside facilitators to lead them through the two-week planning period. The facilitators called a meeting of the staff and lay leaders to assess the information already obtained and to identify key areas to work on. Some of the issues uncovered by the leadership included improving the sense of welcoming in the parish, addressing the need for more physical space, establishing a new evangelization emphasis, providing activities for young adults and fostering greater unity between the parish school and the religious education program.

The facilitators also met individually with each staff member and a number of key individuals from the pastoral council and the coordinating groups. They asked each person the same three questions. "What *could* we be as a parish over the next three to five years?" "What is getting in the way of reaching that ideal?" "How do we get started toward the ideal, what are the first steps?" The accumulated comments from these interviews provided insight into what direction the parish should take over the next three to five years.

Toward the end of the first week of planning all the parishioners were invited to attend a parish town hall gathering. The two hundred people who showed up were separated into small groups and asked these questions: "As we plan for the future, what do we need to hang on to?" "What should we let go of?" "What new things should we initiate?"

"We need to hang on to our good pastor," one person remarked. Another wanted to hold on to recent efforts to revamp the religious education program. A third wanted to be sure to maintain the ten-percent parish tithe that went to aid the poor and needy. Aspects that people were willing to let go of included an unwelcoming attitude among parishioners, resistance to change, bitterness over past decisions, the presence of cliques and in-groups. New things people wanted initiated included publishing the pastor's homilies on the parish website, name tags once a month at the family Mass, connecting with a sister parish south of the border, challenging the youth to contribute financially to the parish.

By this time in the planning process a great deal of information had been collected. The next task was to distill all the data into a report that contained suggestions and insights as viewed from the perspective of the outside facilitators. During the third and final weekend of the two-week process, the staff and lay leaders gathered together to construct a plan for each area of the parish. These included worship, formation, community building, outreach, administration and leadership. This concluded the second of the three steps in the process. Now came the third and most difficult part: implementation.

In drawing up a worthwhile strategic plan, each aspect of the plan should have concrete action steps that can be accomplished over a period of six months to a year. This helps focus people's attention and gives them a sense of accomplishment. Each coordinating group made up action plans that would carry them over the next six months. The task of the staff and council was to monitor the progress of these action steps and to hold groups accountable for what they said they would do. The outside facilitators returned to the parish six months later to assess what was accomplished and what fell by the wayside. This second visit by the facilitators helped keep the planning process on track by affirming progress, renewing interest in the planning project and redirecting failed efforts to assure success in the future.

One success the leaders could affirm came from the community-life coordinating group. Its goal had been to create a more welcoming, friendly spirit in the parish. The first action step was to form a welcoming committee as an outgrowth of community life. After three months, this committee had set up visits to newcomers, taking them cookies and treats, as well as providing them with information about the parish. After four months the welcoming committee had developed a plan whereby each new person or family was matched with a sponsor who showed them around the parish and answered questions. After six months, greeters had been recruited for each of the Masses and people were encouraged to greet one another at the beginning of the liturgies. These were some of the victories one group was able to celebrate with the leadership at the follow-up session.

What this planning process accomplished was a plan of action that would carry St. Mary's over the next three to five years. This, coupled with a yearly tradition of planning, provided them with a process that affirmed their accomplishments. It also kept them focused on what more could be done to respond to the needs of their people, the surrounding area and the promptings of the Holy Spirit in their midst. The core elements of this approach to strategic planning included:

- Gathering information about people's needs and desires, as well as the strengths and shortfalls of all aspects of the parish
- Planning a concentrated period of a few weeks devoted entirely to focusing the information and planning for the future
- Establishing creative, yet realistic goals and action plans that can be measured over time as to their success or failure
- Scheduling a time for an evaluative moment six months after formulating the plan in order to assess what progress has been made, to celebrate the victories achieved and to revitalize those aspects of the plan that had not as yet materialized

(See Parish Evaluation Project listed on p. 180 of References.)

The Discernment Approach

Establishing a yearly cycle of visioning, goals and action steps is only one option for parish planning. This works for the routine situations but not for the extraordinary events or critical decisions that may require a discernment approach. Consider St. Joseph's parish, located on the outer fringes of the city. The town in which it resides considered itself to be a rural hamlet untouched by urban sprawl. Times have changed. The town has been discovered as a quaint, affordable bedroom community. In only a few years, this quiet hamlet, and St. Joe's along with it, is busting at the seams. The church building, which had been adequate for over one hundred years, is now far too small for the new waves of urbanites. Expansion is the obvious choice, but should it remain at the present location or relocate to a section of town where the new homes are being built? This crisis demands a new approach to planning called *discernment*.

Discernment planning begins with the pastoral council appointing a special task force to define the problem and present a possible solution. The task force includes people from more than one coordinating group or ministry, about ten members in all. Their mandate is to investigate all options and to make a recommendation to the council as to the best path to follow. First, however, the task force must do some research. How many new parishioners are expected and, as a result, how big will the church have to be? In what direction will the town grow and what will that mean about the church's location?

Once the situation is well defined, the next step for the task force is to hold open forums for leaders, ministers and parishioners to gather information from all sources about possible options and alternatives. How much extra room will be needed and for what purposes? What costs are associated with each alternative? The task force must also look outside the parish for input, including diocesan offices, regional census data, population trends, as well as information from other parishes that have faced similar circumstances.

After two or three months of information gathering and parish discussions, the task force comes up with a tentative recommendation, along with the rationale for choosing one option over other alternatives. Suppose the task force recommends that the parish buildings be moved to a new location across town. The pastoral council, which includes the pastor, receives this recommendation, makes any necessary refinements and changes, and then presents it to the parishioners for discernment. Care must be taken in making the presentation to the parishioners. The people must realize that this is only a recommendation; no decision has been made. It is still an open issue. The parishioners must also understand that they are not voting on the recommendation. They are being consulted, their wisdom is being assessed. Their ideas will be given to others who will make the final decision.

Going to the people for their input takes three weeks. On the first weekend, the pastor, administrator or task force gives a summary of the proposal at all the Masses and the reasons behind it. Every adult parishioner receives a two- or three-page summary of the recommendation, including the rationale behind it and the proposed costs involved. They also receive a discernment reflection sheet. Over the next week, the parishioners are invited to think and pray over the proposal and to write down all the reasons *against* choosing this recommendation, whether they are in favor of it or not. The following week, the presenters once again speak at all the Masses, encouraging everyone to think and pray over the proposal and come up with all the reasons *for* choosing it. Finally, on the third weekend, they speak again, this time asking for the results of each person's reflection and discernment. Cards are passed out to all the adults. On the card the parishioners are to indicate whether they are for or against the recommendation, along with one reason for their response. The cards are then collected and given to a discernment group for a decision.

A word about the make-up of the discernment group. This is a collection of eight to twelve individuals who are designated as "wisdom people" in the parish. In some cases, this might be the pastoral council, along with the pastor and a few staff members. In other situations it might be a special group chosen for this single task of discernment. It is not the same group as the task force that constructed the recommendation but a separate discerning group organized especially for this purpose. The reason for this is that the task group can become too invested in the proposal to be able to discern freely about what is best for the parish.

Whatever the make-up of the discernment group, its members are present at all the Masses on the third weekend. They are prayed over by the assembly and empowered to discern well for the parish community. They receive the discernment cards and for the next two weeks deliberate among themselves what the best course of action may be. The results of the discernment group are then presented to the council for ratification and to the parishioners for affirmation. In most cases, the decision follows the sentiments of the people. This, however, may not always be the case. Some changes and nuances to the recommendation could be made by the discernment group based on the wisdom and insights of a few wise individuals as recorded on the cards. The majority may not have thought about a particular alternative but once it comes to light it seems as though this is the best path to follow. This is the mysterious and wonderful way the Spirit works through this discernment process.

Once a decision has been made, the action steps should follow immediately. If, for instance, St. Joseph's decides to relocate, then plans are drawn up and a capital campaign begun while interest is still high. Parishes that have used this discernment process are amazed at how generous and supportive parishioners have become during the fund-raising and construction phase once they have been included in the discernment and decision-making phase.

Circular Planning

So far two approaches toward parish planning have been described. One is built around goals and action steps; the other utilizes a discernment approach. Not all parish communities are equipped, or even inclined toward these more linear models of planning. In other situations, a parish might structure itself around coordinating groups that establish goals, but one or other of the ministries, such as the young adults' group or teen ministry, may want to go in a different direction.

A group of pastoral ministers and leaders serving a Native American congregation struggled over a twelve-month period to establish a structure that fit their needs and inclinations. Establishing goals and creating action plans was not working for them. Planning for a long-range future was not their issue; rather, making it through the next week, or even the next day, was their concern.

For them, setting goals made no sense because the environment was too unpredictable and uneven. What initially looks like a good plan gets set aside when someone dies or a crisis occurs. The entire parish community comes to a halt for days as people mourn the deceased or try to cope with the calamity. During this time, special rituals are observed, such as a "give away" of the family's possessions in memory of the person who has died.

After discussing their situation, an alternative planning model was created. They called it *Event-oriented Planning*. This approach acknowledges a more circular reality. One does not establish a desired end point and march off in a straight line to obtain the objective. It is not that simple. At the same time, this model does not surrender a forward direction. Getting there, however, may take many twists and turns. (See Figure 4-A.)

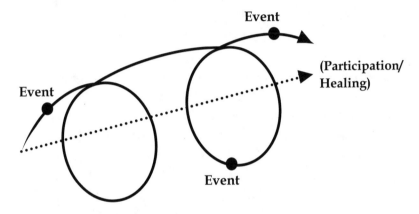

Figure 4-A: Event-Oriented Planning: A Circular Process

Working with the Native Americans and the pastoral ministers serving them, the parish leaders were able to agree on a common focus. One difficulty facing the parish community was encouraging people to participate in church functions, such as Mass attendance, social gatherings and volunteering for jobs and ministries. Part of the reluctance to get involved was the hurt feelings and negative memories the Indians had about the "white man's religion." Times have changed and Native Americans are beginning to discover a blend of ancient rituals and Christian practices, but the hurt still lingers. The common focus agreed upon was to further parish participation by acknowledging and dealing with past hurts, and the process of healing these hurts might render people more willing to participate. The two go hand in hand.

Once the direction was clear, getting there was another matter. It would have to be reached obliquely rather than head-on. This is where the "event-oriented" aspect of planning comes into play. If healing/participation is the direction, then events can be planned that will move the parish community closer to this end. Over the last few years of using this process, some successes are evident. For instance, the teenagers decided to raise money so they could attend a national youth rally in St. Louis. This had never been attempted before. Through much hard work and parishioner support, a group of Native American youth did have a chance to attend. They returned with glowing accounts of the adventure.

For the Jubilee year of 2000, the leaders planned an event that combined the Christian rituals of passing through a Jubilee door of reconciliation and forgiveness with the Native American ritual of burning sage and blessing people with the smoke using an eagle feather. This event helped further healing through their participation in the event.

More often, however, other unplanned events inserted themselves into the lives of the parishioners. Someone dies and everything comes to a halt. Rather than getting stuck in a circle of grief, this event is used as a means toward greater participation and healing. A church building is destroyed by fire or a storm. This, too, becomes an occasion for greater involvement of the community and a path toward greater healing. Some events do seem to stem progress and set the process in a reverse direction. But it is no longer a circle spinning around and around and going nowhere. Instead, it is a spiral heading in a forward direction. It has a purpose. The leaders and the people are beginning to realize that progress is being made. "We are not where we were just six months ago," one person remarked.

Six months is about the extent of the planning time line. Twice a year the staff and leaders reassemble to reflect on what events have occurred and to assess the progress made. They then make plans for the next six months, knowing that only a few of the planned events may take place. That is fine with them. Other unplanned events will surely occur and these can be used in order to achieve greater healing and participation. In the years ahead, another focus may come into view and provide a new direction and orientation, but for now, healing and participation provide all the direction they need.

This circular approach to planning can prove fruitful for other parish situations as well. Working with teenagers, for instance, is usually a circular process. Expecting teens to remain committed to weekly or even monthly attendance may not fit their lifestyle. Choosing one event as a focus could hold more promise. An event such as a citywide, or national or even international youth rally can stir up interest and motivation, as can service projects in poorer areas both within and outside the United States. These events need preparation. Teens spend long hours doing fund-raising, along with background study and preparation. They recruit other teens and publicize the event. This participation, as well as the event itself, can be an experience remembered for a lifetime. The aftermath can be just as rewarding, as the youth tell their story again and again about what it was like and what it meant to them. They cannot help but give witness to how it changed them and changed their outlook on life. As the teens close down one event, the next one is being planned. The spiral continues, as does their own growth and spiritual formation.

Another unexpected outlet for event-oriented planning came to light during the focus sessions with pastors and mentors as they tried to cope with an effective and reasonable workload. (See chapter three.) Much as these pastoral ministers tried to organize their day, they were forever being turned aside by urgent phone calls and impending crises. The pastors spoke of getting to the end of their day with not a single thing from their "To Do" list accomplished. As a help, I presented the circular, event-oriented planning model as one way to view these constant interruptions and find meaning in their disrupted day. I told them to think of one theme or emphasis to concentrate on each day. It might be, for example, adult formation, moral decision making or spiritual growth. This would be a goal or desired outcome to foster among the people the person came in contact with throughout the day. I encouraged them, when they got to the end of their workday, to look back and reflect on how they helped people in the area they wanted to stress. If this happened, whatever the distractions, then it was a worthwhile day for them. With this one emphasis in mind, whenever an interruption or unplanned call or crisis arose, this distraction itself might be an occasion for fostering growth and development in the other person's life.

Consider the pastor who is deep into preparing next weekend's homily. The secretary breaks in to say that a couple needs to see him right away. Keeping in mind the theme for his day was "good moral decision making," he invites the couple in, wondering what this interruption would bring to an already fractured day. They talk about having just come from an ultra-sound test in which they learned that their expected baby will have severe complications. What should they do? They are not planning to end the pregnancy, but they need help coping with this new, unexpected information. Here is a wonderful example of sound, moral judgment. Realizing this, the pastor affirms and supports their choice, putting them in touch with another couple in the parish who had a similar choice to make. The couple now feels blessed to be raising their five-year-old son who has been such a source of happiness to them. When the couple leaves, the pastor returns to his homily preparation with a new sense of awe and appreciation for the deep faith of the parishioners amid the hardships they face. Rather than a distraction, it becomes a help to the homily preparation as well.

A Covenant with the Spirit

Each approach to planning has its own structure and its own way of proceeding. They can be used concurrently or as separate, independent processes. Whatever method is chosen, underlying them all are the common requirements of clear and direct communication, shared vision and decision making, articulation of the group's mission and core values, holding people accountable, opening up the boundaries and providing linkage between groups and individuals.

Jethro counseled Moses to find the best way to lead the Chosen People. To Moses' credit, he "listened to his father-in-law and did all he had suggested." (Exodus 18:24) We must do the same. Listen to the Spirit speaking through the people and follow their advice about what structure and plan to follow. It points a way to a promised land of God's grace and blessings.

An Example of Pastoral Planning
As Manifested by the Leaders and People of
St. Peter's Parish, Dorchester, Massachusetts
By
Rev. John L. Doyle, Pastor

The parish of St. Peter's is located in a congested part of Boston called Dorchester. The worshiping community consists of a group of new arrivals to this country, mostly black, with a smattering of older whites who have decided to stay in the neighborhood. The newcomers bring with them the culture of their native lands, primarily Cape Verde, the Caribbean Islands and Latin America. Most suffer from economic deprivation, the cruelty of racism, the embarrassment of being new arrivals in a strange land. They imitate the passion of Christ in their daily existence.

The community comes together for Eucharist each Sunday to celebrate the great mystery of God's love for us in Christ. Through the Eucharist we are called to incarnate Christ in our lives so as to influence the society in which we are immersed. The goal is the transformation of the structures that control our lives, so as to create a new society, one based on solidarity, justice and dedication to the common good.

Establishing personal relationships, both within the congregation and beyond our membership, is a priority for the parish. A number of individuals have been trained as leaders in the surrounding community. Power is no longer a dirty word for us. We define it as the ability to get things done, as something mandated by the Gospel. What guides our action are the dreams we have for the parish and the wider community. These are some of our dreams:

1. The atmosphere of the Sunday liturgies needs to be welcoming to all who choose to attend, with trained and enthusiastic greeters, pageants, dramas and skits that reflect ethnic customs, as well as parishioners giving faith reflections and witness talks based on their experiences.

2. The parish school needs to be a community that fosters relationships between students, teachers, parents and administrators that

are life-giving. The school not only needs to be integrated more into the total life of the parish but have a mission of outreach to the larger community.

3. The parishioners need to take more ownership for the financial burdens of the parish, sharing what they have, not only in the parish but with those less fortunate than themselves.

4. The parish needs to see itself as an anchor and source of stability for the surrounding neighborhood. It should make its facilities available to all and show a willingness to defend the interests and rights of all. The parish needs to have a reputation for getting involved in issues that are of concern to all area residents, not just parishioners. These include public safety, housing, trash removal and youth. It should work for systemic change and the improvement in the quality of life in the neighborhood.

5. The worshiping community must not be content to stay within the four walls of the church structure but needs to reach out to the homebound, the elderly and the sick. The leadership should empower parishioners in their ministry of care for the poor, the homeless, the abused, the hungry. The parish needs to foster peer ministry of like to like, such as youth to youth, elderly to elderly, Hispanic to Hispanic, and encourage individual initiative in the practice of Christian charity.

To realize our dreams we have made the following plans:

1. We, the leaders, plan to sponsor a parish convention that will focus on the Sunday liturgies. Hopefully this will lead to the training of a new corps of greeters and hospitality ministers for all the Masses.

2. In order to create a better sense of community in the parish school, representatives will be sent to a school-community training program in San Antonio so they can become the trainers and organizers of the school's teachers, students and parents.

3. In the area of financial stewardship, the leadership plans to launch a campaign in order to increase people's use of their Sunday envelopes.

4. For the surrounding neighborhood, the parish will take concrete, practical steps to deal with crime among the youth of the area. Key

parishioners will be chosen to participate in special training sessions related to community organizing and reduction of crime.

5. As for the outreach ministry, the parish staff and leaders will generate a list of homebound elderly and teach family members to bring Holy Communion to these people each Sunday.

The drawback of all these dreams and action plans is that they come from a small core group, that is, pastor, staff and leaders. The next step is to spread the ownership and let others share their dreams and aspirations. The leadership realizes that all good planning must be focused on concrete issues. Given the make-up of the parish, all goals must be immediate, specific and doable.

As a step toward this end, the leadership has decided to sponsor a parish-wide *Event*. This will take place in the parish meeting hall on a Sunday at 2:00 P.M. All the parishioners will be invited to work together in creating a pastoral plan for the parish. They will have a chance to raise issues that are important to them, and to react to the dreams and actions already envisioned by the leadership. In preparation for this event, every member of the parish will receive a survey to assess their attitudes and to spark interest. The pastor, staff and leaders will launch a campaign to "gather the folks" in order to assure a good turnout for the parish gathering. No method for contacting people will be overlooked, including announcements at the Masses over a number of Sundays, one-on-one phone calls and personal visits to those not contacted by other means. The object of all this activity is to have new people attend the parish gathering and to spread the ownership to include more than the present group of active parishioners.

The *Event* is coming in a matter of weeks. It could make all the difference in who we are as a parish community and how we envision our mission to the surrounding area. Whatever happens, it will succeed. This is because Christ is at the core of our adventure. He creates unity among us and turns us into a community. He brings us healing and establishes a reign of justice. He is the one who announces the coming of the new heaven and the new earth.

(St. Peter's Parish is located at 309 Bowdoin Street, Dorchester, Massachusetts, 02122. The phone number is 617-265-1132.)

CHAPTER FIVE

COMMUNAL WORSHIP:
NO ONE WAY

The king read in their hearing
all the words of the book of the covenant
that had been found in the house of the Lord.
The king stood by the pillar and made a covenant
before the Lord . . .
All the people joined in the covenant.

—2 KINGS 23:2–3

The parish is a covenant between God and the people, a place of meeting, a locus of commitment. Communal worship, especially the weekend liturgies, is where this covenant is manifested. It is a joint effort of all God's People assembled to praise, give thanks, seek pardon, gain strength, experience presence, be nourished and ask for what they and others need. There is not one way of doing this. Depending on the environment, the presider, the season of the year and the people present, the liturgy will vary, even within a given weekend. The covenant is an ever-changing, dynamic relationship with God and with one another.

During a class entitled, "Building the Parish from the Ground Up," participants in groups of four or five were asked to fashion a goal for liturgy in a fictitious parish. One small group, in just twenty minutes, produced this goal:

Within the next three years, our liturgies will be welcoming celebrations that invite active participation of the diverse community in such a manner so as to create a hunger to return.

This goal summarizes the aspirations of many people for what liturgy could and should become. It is worth expanding each phrase to explore its meaning.

Welcoming Celebrations

Most parishioners make a conscious choice to attend Mass. Obligation will no longer compel them to come, but a Mass that is welcoming, inclusive, rewarding and meaningful can inspire them to return. From the moment people walk through the doors of the church, they should feel "at home." Everything they encounter, from the environment of the church to the gathered congregation, must speak, "Welcome, come be part of our worship. Be part of our community of faith."

Whether the parish is large or small, this tone of welcoming and acceptance is infectious. I once attended a nondenominational church where I was one among thousands of worshipers. I will never forget the attention given to me, from being guided to a parking place to the welcome at the door. It was not obtrusive or overdone, just respectful and inviting. Contrast this to a small parish where I was one of a few hundred attending Mass. The predominant feeling was aloofness and alienation. No one reached out to me, or to anyone else, for that matter. I was on my own.

First impressions count a great deal. In five to seven minutes people size up the situation and make a judgment about whether the climate is inviting or alienating. That is how much time a parish has to connect with people and invite them in. The presider has much to do with setting the tone. Greeters at the door, compelling music or an inviting and warm environment can all be negated by the staid manner of the priest. "The Lord be with you," can be said in such a way as to mean, "I'm here to do my duty, you're on your own."

If, on the other hand, the priest processes up the middle aisle with a smile, making eye contact with people and then turns to greet the congregation with genuine interest, he sets the tone for what follows. Praying in a manner that conveys the meaning of the prayer, whether of petition or praise, preaching the homily with passion and intelligence, receiving the gifts with gratitude and appreciation; these are the tone-setters that say this is more than a routine celebration. It is a loving encounter, a covenant between God's People and our Creator who is Father/Mother of us all.

The predominant sentiment for creating a welcoming celebration is to *connect, connect, connect.* Each and every person who is present must feel they are special, must know that their presence is appreciated. In one parish at the weekly morning Mass attended by the sixth, seventh and eighth grades from the parish school, the students were sitting in the front pews, arranged according to classes. Spread throughout the rest of the church, and mostly to the back, were the adults who had come to the liturgy.

As part of the greeting at the beginning of Mass, the presider said, "Could I ask a favor of the students in the front? Would you be willing to get up out of your seats and go to the rest of the church and find a partner and then invite that person to be with you for the rest of the Mass? Be gentle. Don't push. See if they will join you."

What happened next was a delight. The students jumped up and scattered throughout the church, finding a friend and bringing the person back to their places. Not everyone took the offer, but most did. Both young and old were full of smiles as they filed into the front pews. No longer were the pews filled with all one size. They had big and little, tall and short, old and young, all mixed up together. As part of the homily, both old and young were asked what the experience had been like for them. One elderly gentleman remarked, "It has been a long time since a young woman has come up and taken me by my arm. Sharing this Mass this morning with her has already become the highlight of my day." An eighth grader said, "This is fun. The Mass is usually kind of boring, but not today." A woman added, "I didn't know we were welcomed up front. I always stayed in back when the students come to Mass."

The next week the students, all on their own, had found a partner and were sitting in the front full of smiles, students and adults alike, as the presider came out to begin Mass. They were connecting with one another, sharing songbooks, joining in the responses, coming up to Communion together. The practice was still going on, to the amazement of the pastor and the delight of the congregation.

Why should this experience of making connections be such a rare experience in Catholic churches? In attending the parishes that do it well, there is a sense of expectation and readiness by the congregation that these connections will be made by the lectors, commentators, music ministers, ushers, greeters, and especially the presiders. Where the connections are not made, people remain isolated and alone. Despite a crowded church, people come and go without ever connecting with the presider, the ministers or the people around them. There may be a perfunctory exchange at the greeting of peace, but it is more of a routine than a connection.

In contrast to this chilly environment, there was a great sense of joy and a welcoming spirit present at a liturgy that took place in a school gymnasium. The Mass was held in this place because the church building was too small to accommodate the large congregation. People entered, having made a name tag for themselves at the entrances. They took their seats, looking around the gathering to see who was there that they might know. Waves and smiles and nods were exchanged as people renewed acquaintances and made connection. It was a family affair with many extended relationships. The opening song began and the priest and ministers approached the altar as waves and greetings continued. When the time for the greeting of peace came, the room was alive with people getting up out of their places and "making the rounds" in order to connect with one another. This Mass was, indeed, a welcoming celebration.

Humor is one sure sign that the connections are being made. When people are happy to be present and delight in worshiping the God of their lives, there is an atmosphere of joy, laughter and celebration. This is far beyond the "joking" stage. This is humor that enjoys one another's presence and a feeling of being "at home" and in a safe, secure environment. People can let down their guards because they are accepted for who they are, saint and sinner all wrapped up in one.

Inviting Active Participation

At one Midwestern parish, on the Sunday between Christmas and New Years at the early morning Mass, I witnessed a remarkable event. Surprisingly, the congregation was very interactive and participative, joining in the responses, the singing, the prayers and the greetings. The singing caught my attention. Two screens on either corner of the sanctuary had words to the music, but each screen had different words. One side of church was singing Silent Night, the other a separate song that harmonized with Silent Night. People sang loudly, obviously enjoying the blend of music they were creating. And this was at the *early* Mass. That is active participation! Obviously the congregation had been invited to do this on a regular basis and they had responded.

So often the opportunity to include the congregation in active participation of the music is lost because those leading it fail to *connect* and *challenge* people to sing. Just raising a hand when it is time for people to join in will not do it. On the other hand, it is so refreshing to be led by someone who relates personally with the congregation and reaches out to each individual to join in the praise of God through song.

At one liturgy, following the greeting of peace, members of the choir spread throughout the church, dividing the assembly into three groups. The congregation knew what was coming and was ready and willing to participate. The song was first sung in unison but then repeated as a round, each section having its turn at the melody. The people sang it four more times, relishing the harmony and their ability to keep their own part. When it was completed, they were obviously proud of their achievement, and approached Communion with a celebrative attitude. Dividing congregations into separate groups of men and women, old and young, right side and left side, front and back, to sing verses to a song can foster active participation. It captures people's attention and gives them a sense of accomplishment and joy in singing.

At the same Mass in the gymnasium mentioned in the previous section, for the final hymn, the leaders of song divided the congregation into four sections: sopranos, altos, tenors and basses. People got out of their seats and gathered into sections and proceeded to sing a beautiful closing song in four-part harmony. Why should this be so unusual? Given the chance, people will participate in creative and active ways in liturgy, rejoicing in praising God and celebrating the sense of community together.

Active participation is the desire of every liturgist, but the invitation and challenge to the congregation is often found wanting. Bishop Kenneth Untener, in an interview for *U.S. Catholic,* said that people often feel like spectators when they attend Mass. "No wonder they feel like spectators, because in many ways that is exactly what they are. They get to speak for 126 seconds in a one-hour Mass, and over half of that is the Creed. You add up every word they say—I tried it with a stopwatch with a video of a Mass—and in a one-hour Mass, 126 seconds is all parishioners have to speak. Except to stand and sit, the first movement they had was the sign of peace, 48 minutes into the Mass. And the only other movement they had was Communion" (*U. S. Catholic*, September 1999, p. 20).

What are some ways to include the congregation in communal worship? At one Mass, for instance, in place of the prepared petitions following the Creed, people were asked to reflect on their coming week and to think of one situation they will be facing that could use some prayers. After spending a moment in reflection, they were invited to turn to the person next to them and ask them to pray for whatever their need was. They were then to listen to the other person's intention and pray for that during the week. It took a few moments for people to catch on, but once they got started, the church was filled with conversations about requests and promises of prayers.

On one occasion when this happened, a liturgy planner was sitting in the back of church. When the invitation was made to share a request for prayers, the person next to her had not been paying attention. When asked what area of her life needed prayers in the coming week, she first was startled and confused. Then she began to weep because she had been thinking of her sister in Guatemala who was sick with cancer. The woman was worried about her and distressed that she could not be at her sister's side in her hour of need. At that moment a bond of caring was established between the liturgy planner and the woman. The two people formed a covenant with each other as they promised to pray for each other's needs.

This simple gesture of encouraging active participation has implications well beyond the simple request for prayers. People return to Mass the next Sunday looking around church for the person they had been praying for all week, wondering how it turned out. It forms bonds of prayer and kinship between total strangers, bonds that are not easily forgotten. This is only one of many ways that could be used to include people in the worship and prayer of the Mass, helping to make the liturgies more attractive and moving experiences for the participants.

One test of a participative liturgy is the way that teenagers or young adults respond. If they feel included and invited to participate, then the liturgy passes the test of active involvement. One parish had a problem with young people losing interest in the liturgy. Their numbers were dwindling. Perhaps a Mass more suited to their tastes would encourage their attendance. The pastor reluctantly agreed to reshaping the Sunday evening Mass to attract this younger clientele, but he said he would do this only for a six-week trial period. A high school music teacher volunteered to lead the music, inviting any young person who could sing or play an instrument to join the new music group. With a great deal of personal contacting and some gentle persuasion, a motley group of thirty people showed up. The "band" included steel guitars, flutes, horns, drums, even violins. All were welcomed to share their talent. Within a few weeks, the music started to gel. It was religious in tone but hardly low key. "Very loud," was the pastor's description. He soon, however, started to catch the spirit and came alive in ways that surprised all who knew him, himself included. People, both old and young, started flocking to the evening Mass. When the music called for clapping, signing and other gestures, people responded. When the music was melodic and meditative, people picked up this mood as well. Young people participated in all the ministries of ushering, reading and distributing Communion. A few even gave witness talks in response to the Scriptures on occasion.

At the end of the trial period, the pastor was amazed at how much had been accomplished in such a short time. He realized that it now had a life of its own. The trial period was over. It had become a regular tradition and active participation was its hallmark. The key figure in making it work was the music director. He, in his quiet way, had the capacity to include divergent gifts and contributions and blend them into a whole. He was able to encourage and attract involvement from not only the band and the choir, but from the congregation as well. What this example indicates is that participation is usually not a problem for the people. It is an issue for the liturgical leadership to solve. People will respond if adequately and appropriately encouraged to do so.

Another way to invite active participation is to work at making the liturgy a moving experience, something that touches the heart and soul of the congregation. It stirs emotions, enkindles faith, reaches deep down inside of people and sends them forth into their daily lives with new resolve, support and zeal. The type of participation at an early Sunday morning Mass may not be as demonstrative as at the Mass for teenagers describe above, but it can be just as involving. Some of the liturgies I have attended as part of silent directed retreats had little music or fanfare, but the level of participation was intense, everyone joining in on a deep level of faith and commitment. Although no words were exchanged among those involved, everyone was aware of one another's presence and was praying for the success of one another's retreat and spiritual journey. Funeral and wedding liturgies often manifest this type of deep involvement, whether in shared grief or tearful joy. People are participating with their whole hearts.

Can this same degree of meaningful, moving participation take place at the regular weekend liturgies? It can, but touching people's hearts is not something that can be turned on at will. It needs careful planning and a prayerful lifestyle by those leading the liturgies. In listening to people read the Scriptures at Mass, for instance, some are moving and others are not. I once witnessed, many years ago, an elderly gentleman who did the first reading on the creation story at the Easter Vigil. He looked out over the top of his glasses at the congregation and told the story of Genesis as if it had never been told before. He was creating the universe right along with God that evening. "And it was evening and morning of the first day." And so it was. People were hanging on his every word. This is an example of active participation.

Bishop Kenneth Untener writes in *Preaching Better*, "The task of all liturgical ministers, including the homilist, is to help the flow of what *Christ* is doing, for Christ is the leader of all liturgical prayer. The first thing we must do when preparing a homily (or planning a liturgy) is to stand humbly before the Lord." Some homilists and liturgical ministers have the gift of touching hearts, and people respond by actively participating in worship. Deep speaks to deep. If those leading liturgy are people of prayer and are in touch with the Spirit's work in their lives, then their liturgical ministering will be authentic and moving to the congregation. On the other hand, if someone puts on a show, no matter how devout it may appear, it will not have the same impact or serve to encourage people to become involved in worship.

The Diverse Community

One size does not fit all. People come in many shapes and sizes, with many different desires and needs. Parishes must be willing to ask the parishioners what style of worship would interest them and to experiment with different models. Can this be done within the present directives for liturgy? My observation of the motivation and creativity of the Spirit-filled People of God convinces me that it can. The alternative is a shrinking assembly as people seek other places and options for worship. These other places may be large nondenominational churches or small, intimate communities of faith. They target special needs and interests. This is the secret to their success. Catholic parishes can learn much from this approach. One place this is happening is in multi-cultural Catholic parishes. The weekend liturgies are in many languages, with diverse music, customs and rituals. This diversity puts a strain on the presiders to keep adjusting to these various styles of liturgy, but adjust they must or they will be facing empty pews and a dwindling congregation.

If this is the case in multi-cultural parishes, why not in more homogeneous ones as well? The homogeneity is only on the surface. Underneath people long for their own expression of worship. The various weekend liturgies must be manifestations of diverse tastes and preferences. The apostles and disciples that followed Jesus, both women and men, were a diverse community, varying in age, background, place of origin and preferences. Yet Jesus spoke in ways that were inclusive of all, accepting each person as unique and gifted. This should be the spirit of modern-day liturgies as well.

Practically, this will mean getting in touch with the diversity and uniqueness of each Mass, trying to discover the preferences and disposition of each group of worshipers. One Mass may represent a more traditional group, another a family spirit with younger children, a third a young-adult crowd with singles and newly married couples. Once the special character of each Mass is ascertained, then the liturgical planners must shape the liturgical style and symbols to fit that particular group. This stretches the capabilities of the planners. It suggests that each liturgy may need its own set of liturgical coordinators and planners, along with input from those attending each Mass. In this way the liturgies become a pastoral partnership. No single group of leaders or liturgical organizers will be enough. A worship committee or coordinating group might oversee the planning as a whole, but each liturgy would be directed and planned by its own group. This group would pay close attention to the unique character of the congregation and invite active participation in a way that best fits that particular worshiping community.

Diversity can be celebrated within the same liturgy as well. As happens in a number of parishes, one weekend Mass may include sign language for the deaf. In one parish, that particular liturgy was a celebration of deafness. At the Alleluia before the Gospel reading, the entire congregation signed the acclamation, making the deaf community a more integral part of the Mass. At Communion time, every Eucharistic minister not only said the words "The Body (Blood) of Christ," but signed them as well, not just for the deaf but for the entire community. More and more parishes are including music that has verses in more than one language, in English and Spanish, for instance. Choirs do a mixture of music, including gospel music, traditional hymns and modern songs. All of this is a way of saying, "There is room for everyone. No one is being excluded. We are Christ to one another. Jesus is present not only in the bread and wine, but in the Scripture, in the symbols and gestures we use, and especially in one another. We, in all our unique diversity, bring Christ to life in the respect, acceptance and love we show to each and every person present in this community."

One concrete example of this acceptance of diversity was an Easter Sunday morning liturgy at an inner-city parish. The church was filled with balloons and streamers, with people of every color and background, all rejoicing in the Risen Christ. A number of those in front had limited mental capabilities, but this did not prevent them from celebrating with both soul and body. They danced and sang and shouted for joy, sometimes at the most unexpected times during the Mass. The rest of the congregation did not mind. This was part of what it means to be the full Body of Christ. It was a living example of a diverse community that was comfortable celebrating together. The motto of the Mass was, "Come as you are; all are welcome here."

Creating a Hunger to Return

The obligation to attend Mass does not motivate people as it once did. There must be an inner desire and a personal longing to return to church. One liturgy planning committee had as its goal that "everyone who attended the weekend Masses said as they were leaving, 'Wow, I want to come back to that!'" For some, what enticed them back was the thought-provoking and challenging homilies. For others, it was the inspiring music or the sense of community, the welcoming atmosphere or the sense of the sacred and holy. Whatever the cause, those who attended felt compelled to return.

There is a sense of awe and mystery to good liturgy that goes beyond the efforts of the presider or the ministers. The operation of Christ's Spirit is active in each individual who attends, and this has an impact on all that takes place. Their faith is nourished and their lives are blessed by their attendance, no matter what happens at Mass. But the way the Mass is celebrated and the style of the liturgy also has an influence. Some liturgies are more appealing and encourage repeated attendance to a greater extent than others. What makes the difference? Besides being welcoming celebrations and making connections with people, besides being inclusive and moving experiences, besides inviting active participation, two other ingredients will draw people back to church. People will return if they find the liturgies to be both *nourishing* and *challenging*.

First, nourishing. Does what happens at Mass connect with people's everyday lives and give them sustenance for the strains and struggles they face? The way the liturgy is celebrated, the way the Word is broken open during the homily, the way people are affirmed and supported and included in the prayer of the community: All these aspects of the Mass must relate to people's daily experience. Are they given real food and drink, nourishment for adult believers, rather than pablum better suited for infants in the faith? People come to worship from many walks of life, carrying a collection of cares and concerns. How will the mother facing a depressed and anxious teenager at home find the strength at Mass to be understanding and patient with her child? How will a husband who is coping with his wife's treatments of breast cancer find the right words of encouragement and hope? How will a couple dealing with the pain of their adult children who are undergoing divorce find solace? How will a single woman learn to cope with loneliness by participating in the Eucharist? Does anyone care when and how these people attend church? Do the readings, reflections, community support or communal prayer provide individuals with the will and determination to face life's hurts and heartaches with equanimity and grace? Are there aspects of the liturgy that people can carry home with them that will provide support and solace for the coming week? These are the questions that should be going through the priest's and ministers' minds and hearts as they prepare for and preside at the liturgy. If people discover nourishment and sustenance for their everyday lives during Mass, they will, indeed, have a hunger and thirst to return.

A second aspect of liturgy that will draw them back is a sense of challenge and accountability. The Mass should not be just a "feel good" experience. People need to be confronted by the demands of the Gospels. They should experience the joyous yet uneasy feeling of disciples sent forth on a mission. The purpose of the Mass is to challenge people to "Go out and spread the Good News, healing one another" (Mark 16:18).

This accountability has many facets. One is to call people to become evangelizers in their everyday lives. Imagine what it would look like if, at every Mass, the rallying cry was, "You are the grace-bearers. Take the Good News to those who really need it the most, those in your homes, offices, malls, freeways and airports. Practice the Gospel readings, share a peace greeting, extend Eucharist, be church to those you meet. We will help you. We will listen when you return to tell us what happened. We will accept whomever you bring back with you to our liturgical gathering. We are behind you, but it is in your hands. No one else can touch the people you will interact with this day, this week, this month. May God be with you, as we are with you in spirit."

In order to get across this emphasis of being ministers in people's everyday lives, of accepting a personal responsibility to be an evangelizer, the liturgies must not only be inward looking, taking care of personal needs, but directed outward as well. We are not placed on earth as Christians just for ourselves; we are here primarily for others.

As a way of getting this across to a congregation, consider the parish that at the end of Mass one weekend, passed baskets around the church which contained brand new gold dollars. For those who wished, they were asked to exchange a gold dollar coin with a paper dollar from their own pockets. The task was to take that one coin and do something kind and helpful to another person during the week. "Come back next week," they were told, "and tell us what you did. No speeches please, just a one-minute witness." Many took up the challenge. The shared homily at the next weekend liturgy was memorable. One person gave the coin to a waitress as part of a tip, just to surprise her. Another gave it to a homeless person as an extra bonus when she took her turn at the soup kitchen. A third gave it to the tooth fairy to put under the pillow of his daughter. A fourth gave it to the attendant at a toll booth, paying for his own toll and for the car behind him. The stories of generosity and gift went on and on, delighting the congregation, until finally the presider brought the witnessing to a close. Since then, it has become an annual event whenever the Gospel of the talents is read at Mass.

Another facet of challenging people is to call them to greater simplicity of lifestyle. The temptation is to think that the more one has, the safer or happier or healthier they will be. This is a myth. The more possessions one has, the more worries and concerns they bring with them. John the Baptist told the people who came to him seeking advice to take one of the two coats they had and "share with anyone who has none; and whoever has food must do likewise" (Luke 3:11). The question for those planning and leading liturgies is, "Does the ritual we call Eucharist challenge people to simplify their lives and seek a way of acting that is modeled on people rather than things, on opening up to the needs of others rather than concentrating on one's own concerns and desires?"

A homily recently focused on "stuff." It began with people's experience of moving from one home to another, something we do many times in our lives. This is the occasion for throwing out all the extra "stuff" we have accumulated since the last move. Garage sales are filled with this extra "stuff," dumpsters are overflowing with last year's "stuff." The homilist paused with each new example, waiting for the congregation to fill in the blanks with the "stuff" they had lying around the house, office, garage or cottage. These are our material possessions, but our minds and hearts are filled with just as much "stuff" as our homes. Worthless images from television, radio, Internet, videos fill our heads. These both bore us and tantalize us. How to clear our lives and our minds of all this "stuff" in order to discover what has true and lasting value. One person came up after Mass to thank the homilist, but the man was also shaken by the experience. "Do you think I should let go of my boat? It is some of the 'stuff' that fills my leisure time that perhaps could be put to better use. I know this is not for you to answer, but it gives me pause."

The world of "virtual reality" is beginning to take hold in this country. People flock to virtual theme parks which are buildings filled with virtual rides and thrills, all done with electronic sensors and headsets. There is one such theme park in downtown Chicago where a family was in a rubber raft trying to "shoot the rapids." They were ducking what they supposed was splashing water from the river, and they were paddling with great energy and effort to miss the rocks and waterfalls. But there was no water anywhere to be found. It was all just make-believe. What an excellent symbol for the direction that a large part of the American culture is heading. It is built on appearances and images, not on substance. Will those who attend liturgies in Catholic parishes discover the substance and truth of Christ's message and presence? If they do, they will experience a hunger to return. If not, they will be tempted to give in to the virtual reality of the culture and continue to search, perhaps in all the wrong places, for rituals and experiences they hope will bring them life.

The reading from the Second Book of Kings that began this chapter has this added description of the king entering into a covenant with Yahweh. "The king stood by the pillar and made a covenant before the Lord, to follow the Lord, keeping his commandments, his decrees, and his statutes, with all his heart and all his soul, to perform the words of this covenant that were written in this book. All the people joined in the covenant" (2 Kings 23).

This is the proof of a successful liturgy, that it calls people into a loving covenant with God and with one another, that it challenges them to remain faithful to God's call of loving service, and fills them with a desire to stay connected with the wellspring of grace, the Spirit within and the Christian community gathered in celebration of Christ's presence.

Aspects of Good Liturgy
As Experienced by a Pastoral Administrator
from the Diocese of Saginaw, Michigan
By
Sr. Virginia Scally, SNDdeN

I have served as a pastor(al administrator) for over nine years. Because the majority of parishioners' only experience of parish is at the weekend Masses, it is critical that the liturgy enables the people to worship the God of their lives. They need to do this both intimately as individuals and communally as part of the worshiping assembly. People are hungry for this spiritual sustenance.

Many aspects of the liturgy can nourish and sustain parishioners. The first and most important aspect of liturgy that worked for me was good preaching. Prayerfully and creatively breaking open the Word can speak effectively to people's everyday lives. It can help them recognize the sacred dimensions or potential of their lives, lives that are usually filled with the details of a busy and demanding secular world. Those attending church desire and need a way to connect with God. Good preaching that breaks open the Scriptures in a way that helps them to see the deep down connections between the Lord's words and ways of living and their own is so appreciated. The People of God leave the Table of the Word and the Table of the Eucharist with concrete memories of nourishing "bread" that will help them live as God's witnesses in the world.

Ideally, good preaching is the fruit of a week which makes a priority of daily study and reflection, of prayer and listening that considers the Word, the particular community to which I'm preaching and the action of the Spirit. It is a sacred privilege and a sacred responsibility that I assume. If the message is prepared from one's depths, then the people will be nourished. This has worked for me and it has worked for my people.

Another component of the liturgy that has worked for me is good liturgical music. I have discovered this from both the presence of good music and from its absence. I don't mean just *having* music at the Mass. I mean making liturgical music a priority. This includes having someone salaried to be in tune, not with what music is available in the missalette, but in tune with the best contemporary liturgical musicians who are writing music for the various liturgical seasons.

I would make the securing of an excellent keyboard person a priority as well. I have found that there are powerful songs available for Catholic liturgy, most of which are user-friendly so that once learned, the congregation can participate fully and claim the music as its own. I am talking about music that everyone sings, music that speaks to the soul, that nourishes, supports and challenges people in the living out of the paschal mystery, that inspires people and makes them one in song and worship. Having qualified and gifted leaders of music is worth the effort and costs. This can make a significant difference for that one hour a week the parish has to touch people's lives in a meaningful way.

Another ingredient of liturgy, one that extends beyond the church building, is visiting parishioners in their homes, sitting around their kitchen tables over a cup of coffee or tea. It is so easy to get too busy and ignore this part of Eucharist. While people so appreciated my efforts to recognize them and call them by name, I discovered that this was not enough for me. Twice I had a chance to spend some extended time in the home of a parishioner that I thought I knew, only to discover that there was so much more richness and depth to the person than I had ever realized.

I came away from the home saddened by my own previous deprivation. My preaching could have spoken so much more deeply to people's experience if I had spent more time visiting with them one on one. I would have known my parishioners more closely, which would have enabled me to be a more effective pastor and shepherd. I would have seen the deeper beauty in more of my people's eyes. Now, more than ever, as the world becomes computerized and less personal, that kind of personal knowing makes a difference. The challenge is to make this personal visiting in homes a pastoral priority. There never will be time for it. So just do it! It could make a significant difference in the quality of one's ministry and the nourishment people receive when they attend liturgy.

These, then, are the aspects of liturgy that nourish and sustain people's lives — good preaching, inspiring music and personal contact with people's everyday lives. This is the "bread" that brings Eucharist to life.

(Sr. Virginia Scally, SNDdeN had been a pastoral administrator at St. John the Baptist Parish, located at 545 Mapleridge in Carrollton, Michigan 48724, and served two parishes in central Michigan: St. Paul the Apostle in Ithaca, and St. Martin De Porres in Perrinton. She is presently preparing for pastoral ministry in Lima, Peru.)

CHAPTER SIX

TAKING THE PARISH TO THE PEOPLE:
BRIDGING GAPS

I will make for you a covenant on that day . . .
I will betroth you to me forever;
I will betroth you to me in righteousness and in justice,
In steadfast love, and in mercy.
I will betroth you to me in faithfulness;
And you shall know the Lord.

—HOSEA 2:18, 19–20

The best parishes are founded on relationships, connecting people with people and fostering bonds between them. This connecting happens during the weekend liturgies and after each Mass as people share refreshments and companionship. It happens at meetings when people not only conduct business but share stories and prayer together. It happens at staff and council gatherings at which the leadership models community by the care and concern they have for each other. It happens when people reach out beyond their own groups and invite others to their activities. It happens in formation programs where people not only learn about their faith but encounter a supportive community that helps them on their way. It happens when the poor and the needy are not just "causes" or "case studies" to be assisted but individuals who deserve respect and seek companionship. These are the relationships that form a parish into a loving community of believers and followers of Christ.

Forming community, however, is a hard sell in American society where autonomy and independence are so highly prized. At the same time, people long to be "in touch" with one another, but often on their own terms. The popularity of cellular phones reveals the need for people to be contacted, but they hold on to the freedom to initiate a call or to hang up. Challenging people to live and think communally is no easy task.

There is a small group of Catholic couples who at one time attended church regularly and were involved in parish activities and ministries. Their children are now grown, and they no longer feel obligated to attend their parish on a regular basis. It simply does not fit their needs. These couples have moved "beyond that stage," as one person put it. The group meets monthly to discuss current social and religious issues. They still go to church occasionally, but this does not have the same meaning or impact it once had for them. They are not active in parish functions and don't feel their insights and experiences are valued by the present parish leadership.

Not many of my thirty-seven nephews and nieces attend church regularly, although almost all still consider themselves Catholics. They, like many other younger adult Catholics, find little about church or in their local parishes that touches their lives and encourages their participation.

The Urban, Modern Context

Reverend Jack Linnan, a professor at Catholic Theological Union in Chicago, gave a talk at the annual convention of the National Federation of Priests' Councils in May 1996. The focus was on the Catholic parish, which he described as an outdated, largely agrarian model existing in a modern, urban environment. Its members move from one world into another when they attend church and parish functions.

Catholic parishioners are as modern and urbanized as any other Americans. They live in a functional, computerized, constantly moving world. Boundaries are blurred. The automobile, television set, computer, Internet connection and cellular phone have inserted them into a geography that is independent of neighborhood and local culture. The Catholic parishioner, like any other American, seeks efficiency and standardization. The common theme is, "I want this thing to work. I do not have time to mess around. I'm willing to pay if it's worth the money." One practical symbol of this modern, urbanized context is the television remote control;

whoever holds it has control. "Options" is the name of the game, as many and as quickly as possible.

Take these modern, urbanized people and place them in a Catholic parish. They are faced with a very different reality. "You belong to *this* parish because you live within its boundaries." There are often limited options to their membership in the parish, be it the types of Masses it offers, the formational programs it provides for themselves or their children or the areas of involvement associated with their age group and interests. There are few alternatives, little variety and no control. They encounter two different worlds: their personal life and their church life.

Father Linnan suggests two other aspects of the current social climate that militate against parish involvement. One is the marginalized character of American churches. Unfortunately, what spells success in many aspects of our culture is still associated with a male-oriented world. Large corporations, the stock market, sports are all dominated by male images. The role of women is often relegated to a nurturing, educating, ministering domain. This phenomenon occurs in the churches as well. Pastoral ministry becomes a woman's thing.

Kenneth Woodward voiced the same theme in an article published in the November 22, 1996, issue of *Commonweal* entitled "Gender and Religion." "My concern," he writes, "is not with theory or theology but with the atmosphere of ordinary American churches as I find them. And what I find in them is that gradual disappearance of anything that might adequately be described as masculine." This feminization of organized religion contributes to the attitude that church attendance and parish involvement are nonessential aspects of people's lives, relegated to the private sphere. Moving up the socio-economic ladder has little to do with church or parish identity. These could even be a deterrent or, at the very least, a distraction from one's *real* goals in life.

Another aspect of the modern, urban context that makes parish involvement difficult, according to Father Linnan, is the increasingly unreflective nature of American life. There is little time in our busy schedules to reflect on *anything*. At home, in our cars and in the marketplace, television, newspapers, radios and computers feed us the news, analyze it and interpret it for us. These channels of information instruct us with flash images, fast talk and clipped sound bites for quick consumption. Catholic parishes can fall victim to this non-reflectiveness. "Don't confuse me with the facts," becomes the cry. "Tell me what to believe, what to think, what to choose. Stick to the basics. Processing the data is your job. Just give me the results of your analysis." This anti-intellectual, non-reflective mood is creating a country of nonthinkers. Asking people to get beyond the labels and sound bites is too demanding.

Enter the American Catholic parish, an outdated model in a new era. Though the rhetoric may not voice it, the typical parish is still a top-down organization that seeks to draw its members from a defined area within concrete boundaries. The parish demands regular attendance at Mass, involvement in classes to receive first sacraments and financial support through weekly contribution of envelopes. But the parishioners come from a different mold. They are, in general, critical of central authority and power, desirous of change and options and are not tied down to one locality. They are members of many diverse groups and organizations. They view organized religion as on the fringe of their lives, far down their list of priorities and interests, one of many activities vying for their attention.

But wait. Perhaps there is a deeper reality at work in this clash of outdated parish models and modern, urbanized realities. Jesus is still alive and present in this changing and complex world. How would he respond to this dichotomy of Church and daily life? To judge from his public life, Jesus would be with the people, including those on the fringe. The Gospel shows him as one who sought out the lost, befriended the non-attenders, liberated the marginalized, set even the most hardened hearts on fire and proclaimed God's universal love and mercy to the lonely and the rootless. He connected with people's real lives and captured their imaginations. Can the extension of Jesus's ministry in today's world—the Church and the parish—do anything less?

I believe the local parish still has a chance for survival, but only if it changes its focus from "in here" to "out there." Shift the emphasis from bringing people to the parish to taking the parish to the people. Change the goal from greater parish involvement to helping people live a full, human life in the modern world. Let's admit that many who are no longer coming to church are still spiritual, grace-filled people who are searching for meaning and fulfillment in their lives. Parishes have to find new ways to connect with these individuals through the Internet, e-mail, media, personal visits and direct contact. To the leaders and active parishioners, I say, "Put yourself in their shoes and see the parish from their eyes, not your own." What does the parish look like from the outside? Is it welcoming, inclusive, attractive, nonjudgmental, not condemning? Does it offer solace to those who are struggling with business ventures, difficult children, overspending, caring for elderly parents? For many, the parish is irrelevant and incidental to these daily struggles.

Consider Marilyn, a baptized Catholic who no longer attends church. Both she and her husband do not belong to a parish but they still call themselves Catholics. With the birth of their first child and the challenges associated with parenting, she longs to discover a place of worship and a community to call home. She looks on from a distance, wondering how to make the first move, afraid and anxious to take the first step back to church. Or consider Richard, a conscientious and caring Catholic with two young sons. His wife works on Sundays and it is up to him to take his children to church. But after a long, draining workweek he does not have the energy or desire to sit through a service where his children are not likely to remain quiet and his own patience will be tested. What hope does the parish hold out to these two and myriads like them? Let us consider a number of aspects of parish life to see what options are possible that speak to urban, modern Catholics. These aspects include building relationships and bonds between people, providing for their formation in the faith, reaching out in service to those in need and connecting with those on the fringe.

Building Relationships

Assumption parish is up to date in most everything it offers, but something is missing. It has gotten into a routine of weekend liturgy, Wednesday night religious formation and monthly committee meetings. One person mentioned at a staff meeting that perhaps the parish had forgotten how to have fun together. "When is the last time we went out as a staff just to enjoy ourselves? When have the council and committees had a social night together? Maybe the parish should reinstate those dances, picnics and ice cream socials of the past." Another staff member retorted, "Those events fell into disuse because no one could be found to plan them." Nevertheless, the staff agreed to bring it up at the next pastoral council meeting. When this happened, the council gave the suggestion of more social events a cautious but positive response. The community life committee was given the task of exploring options for doing this. Its mandate was to set up a yearly tradition of fun events, ones that fit the lifestyles and busy schedules of both volunteers and parishioners. "Spread the planning so that no one group is given too much to organize and plan," the committee was told. The council went on to say, "Be sure to enlist new people, those who have not been involved before. And above all, everyone should have fun doing it. This is not for making money but for building relationships."

The committee members set about their task with energy and vigor. "Something for everybody," was their motto. Making up a schedule of monthly socials was a fun event in itself. The annual picnic in August would start off the year. This was a celebration of the parish's feast day, the Assumption, and included an outdoor Mass, games, a potluck and dancing. It was well organized and had a good following. The women's club and K of Cs did a great job getting it together and it included all parish groups and ministries. Don't tamper with something that is working.

September would be a bike trip for young and old. A route could be mapped out that might begin after the last Sunday morning Mass at the parish. People would come to Mass dressed for the event. They would then follow back roads and bike trails to a place where refreshments would be provided. People would be encouraged to relax and enjoy one another's company. Then they would ride their bikes back to the parish by a different route. What a nice way to celebrate the start of school and the end of summer.

A "Taste of Assumption" would be a fun event for October. People would bring special dishes that reflect their place of origin and ethnic identity. Booths could be set up, each representing a different part of the world and featuring food and drink unique to that region. This is where new people could be called in, inviting them to bring a dish or dessert, to connect with a booth appropriate to their heritage. Bring what you can and share in the feast.

November is a time of thanksgiving. Throughout the year parishioners bring food stuffs to the Masses as a concrete way of helping the needy. This could be a time to celebrate their generosity and keep the poor in mind as well. The weekend before Thanksgiving might be a huge "give away" ritual. The Native Americans do this as part of their funeral rites. They give away their possessions as a remembrance of the deceased. The parishioners at Assumption could do the same, only as a celebration of all the blessings received from God. Not only would they contribute to the food baskets, they would bring some of their possessions, even treasured ones, and invite anyone who wishes, especially those in need, to come and pick out whatever they want. There could even be people volunteering to deliver the larger items, such as computers, furniture and television sets, to homes and agencies. Surprise packages could be given away as door prizes. It would be similar to the traveling antique show on public television, only this would cover a full range of goods and possessions.

The committee felt that an annual Christmas card party should be inaugurated for the first or second week of December. On Sunday afternoon, parishioners would be invited to bring the Christmas cards they would be mailing out and to enjoy the afternoon writing their friends and relatives. This could all be done in a festive environment of Christmas music and snacks. Baby-sitting would be provided as an incentive for people to come.

January might include a Super Bowl party, complete with refreshments and "play money" for betting on the game. Everyone is given money as they come in and that can be disposed of in whatever way they wish. Those with the most "cash" at the end receive prizes. A number of large-screen televisions could be scattered around the room, along with ballots for the best and worst commercials. People would be encouraged to bring their favorite snacks and refreshments, baby-sitting, of course, would be provided, free of charge.

A Valentine's Day dinner dance could be the focus for February, complete with special rituals such as celebrations of marriage anniversaries, remembrance of loved ones, along with music featuring each decade since the middle of the last century. People would be encouraged to dress according to a particular era so that one table would feature a fifties motif, another the sixties, and so on.

March might be a celebration of St. Patrick's and St. Joseph's feast days all wrapped up into one glorious evening of storytelling and humor. Everyone would have a maximum of two minutes to tell a story or a joke. The meal would be a potluck, a covered-dish affair split up into courses. Each course of the meal would have twenty minutes of jokes and stories before it, ten people for each course. Microphones would be spaced throughout the hall to keep it moving. At the end of each session, the audience would vote on the best joke or story. Once the dinner is completed, as many as fifty people might have had a chance to participate. At the end, all the winners would come up for a bow and a final word before the conclusion of the evening. And a good time was had by all.

Easter would be the focus for April and with it a church full of those who may not attend regularly. How can this be a celebrative event for all involved? The priests, musicians and liturgical ministers are usually worn out after the services of Holy Week and the Easter Vigil. What will bring life to the community on Easter morning? An invitation to breakfast the Sunday after Easter might do it. Volunteers would circulate throughout the church before the Masses asking new people and infrequent attendees to sign the parish guest book. Each person who signs the book is given a ticket to a special free breakfast to take place the next Sunday. It would be cooked and served by those under thirty-five. It is the young people's way of saying thanks to all the hard-working "older" parishioners who keep the parish running smoothly throughout the year. It could also be a celebration of new people who are drawn into the event by attending the Easter Masses.

May might feature a song and dance night, including different types of dancing, from folk to modern, and different styles of songs, Broadway to rock. People would have a chance to learn new steps and new songs, and teach others what they themselves have to offer. No wallflowers could withstand the pull of the dance floor or the lure of a melody, no matter how inadequate they might feel. People would be asked to bring their favorite songs and try them out. Prizes would be awarded to those providing the best and most unique contributions.

June could be Casino Night. "No-Risk Gambling" might be the slogan. No one loses. Those who attend receive a packet of play money when they arrive. They are free to play cards or blackjack at the tables set up for this purpose. When the evening comes to an end, those with the most money receive prizes for their good luck.

Reflecting on the urban, modern lifestyle of the parishioners, the July event is a "non-event," at least as a gathering of the parishioners. It takes place via e-mail and letters. Each parishioner is invited to design a road trip, one, two or three days round trip by car. Each trip would leave from and return to the front steps of the church. These itineraries could be posted on the walls of the vestibule or on the parish website. People would be encouraged to try them out sometime during the summer months as possible trips for the family. Each entry would be assigned a number. At the end of the summer, one entry is drawn out to receive the grand prize of a trip to

Europe for the entire family using frequent-flyer miles donated by parish-ioners. Those who try out the trips are asked to give a brief account via e-mail or letter of what they did and how they enjoyed the trip. The most creative description would also be given a prize. The purpose of this "non-event" is to use the ideas and creativity of the people as an encour-agement to use one's leisure time well.

Once the year's events had been mapped out by the community life committee, the next task was to find people to plan and run them. The committee began by personally contacting twenty-four people to be the co-chairs of these activities, two people per monthly event. As long as people knew they had only one activity a year to plan, and that they did not have to do it alone, that they were guaranteed a group of workers to put it on, they readily agreed to assume this task. Next, the committee made up a schedule of events and published it in the bulletin and parish newsletter. Then they put large sheets of paper on the walls of the church's gathering space with a time line for the preparation of each event. They talked at all the Masses and asked people to help plan just one event for the coming year in order to make it a success. Parishioners were encour-aged to ask their friends and family members to sign up as well, whether or not they attended church. These volunteers were led by each event's co-chairs and were to start planning for it at least two or three months before it was to take place.

A special committee of phone callers was established to operate throughout the year. This group of eight to ten people was asked to make five calls a month to parishioners who were not active in any parish organ-ization or ministry. The task was simple: to ask those they telephoned to bring a covered dish, dessert or refreshment to the monthly social event. This was an attempt at enticing inactive members to become involved.

This was the way in which the Assumption parishioners began to have fun together as a parish. Of course, many other things were going on in the parish that helped build relationships. The weekend liturgies were communal gatherings, both during and after the Masses. Weddings and funerals continued to draw people together as a community as people cel-ebrated with one another. Other ministries and activities helped foster bonds between people. What these monthly fun events did, however, was to provide a regular occasion for people of different ages, backgrounds and levels of parish involvement to come together as a community and to enjoy one another's company. They ate, drank, laughed, danced, sang and played together. America's fast-paced culture does not provide these occasions in the ordinary run of people's lives. As was said at the beginning of this chapter, the best parishes are founded on relationships, connecting people with people and fostering bonds between them. This is one of many ways it could happen.

Forming Faith

In seeking ways to help form people in their lifelong journey of faith, let's admit that few adults will come to educational talks or presentations. Most are also reluctant to sign up for a small Christian community. In the midst of an overactive, over-extended work, family and play week, the investment is just too great. Other ways of connecting with adults must be found. What will stir their hearts? What will get their attention? What will motivate them to grow in their faith?

For those who come to Mass on the weekend, one option is to add a short period of faith formation at the end of Mass. One pastor used a two-minute egg timer, putting it up on the lectern just before the final blessing. He announced that he would take no more than two minutes to answer any questions people might have about the Mass, the Church or their faith. "I have put a box in the gathering space," he said, "along with a pen and paper. I will select one entry each week. No need to say who you are. I can't promise I will know the answer but I will give it a try. I can't do too much harm in just two minutes." The response from parishioners was cautious at first, but once people saw he was serious about sticking to the two minutes, and heard the pithy responses he gave to the questions, the entries came flooding in. They ranged from questions about the Bible and Church teachings, to curiosities about why water is added to wine at Mass and what saints were depicted in the stain glass windows of the church. It became an eagerly awaited conclusion to the liturgy, especially to see if he could do it before the timer went off. He sometimes had to stop in the middle of a sentence if the bell rang. The pastor himself found it rewarding. "I have had to do some homework to discover the answers but at least it keeps people from leaving early."

Some parishes in the Saginaw diocese have been using this technique for adult formation. They call it "four-minute teaching" at the end of Mass. Many of those attending Mass, the leadership discovered, were relatively illiterate about Church traditions but were eager to know more. One parish spent the time each week describing the sacraments. Another took each phrase of the Creed and another had the congregation pick the topic for the next week. It was not necessarily the presider who gave the four-minute teaching. It might be a staff person or a parish leader who had studied the topic for that week. It brought the issues to the people in a way they could understand and learn from the experience.

Another way to stir people's hearts and encourage their growth in faith is to begin with the children. It is a tried-and-true method of parental engagement. The typical parish model is to have the parents deposit their children at religious education classes and have them return to church to pick them up afterwards. The parents feel ill equipped to provide religious formation for their children. "Let the Church do it, but keep me out of it," they say. What will get the parents involved? What fits their fast-paced, non-reflective world?

Some parishes use weekend liturgies as the starting point, but they also insist that parents be the primary religious educators of their children. With this in mind, every Mass starts with an invitation to the children to go to their own room for lectionary-based catechesis during the first part of the liturgy. When they return to the congregation they have in hand take-home materials and projects that assist the family throughout the week. The parents have their own study guides as a resource. It is a weeklong learning experience for the whole family. This is only one of many creative approaches for bridging the gap between Church and everyday life without demanding attendance at adult formation classes or presentations. Take the parish to the people, not the people to the parish.

Such an approach would shift the focus away from established classes to open learning models that stress dialogue, relationships and at-home activities. The parish provides the framework, resources and encouragement for spiritual development, for family growth and ministry in the workplace, for integrity in moral decision making. It seeks to relate to the non-reflective nature of modern living and to restore people's faith in an institution that has been pushed far to the background.

The Church is still searching for ways to do this. One option would be to challenge families to establish one at-home night each week. This would include a meal in common and "fasting" from television for the evening. One parish supplied families with a special sign to tape over the front of the TV set that read, "Off limits for home night." Another option would be to set up tables after Mass for various occupational groupings. People would gather in clusters according to jobs and discuss how to bring Church into their workplace during the coming week. Staffs might also visit work sites of parishioners and experience firsthand what issues and circumstances people face in trying to be ministers on the job. Such exposure would provide a wealth of material for preaching and presentations, not to mention endorsement of the value of people's work. This is one way in which to connect the parish with the everyday lives of the parishioners.

Adult Formation

The American bishops have produced a plan called *Our Hearts Were Burning Within Us* for adult formation with these goals:

1. Invite and enable ongoing conversion to Jesus in holiness of life
2. Promote and support active membership in the Christian community
3. Call and prepare adults to act as disciples in mission to the world

These are lofty goals but they are difficult to implement in a modern, urban climate. Ongoing conversion is a challenge when people are non-reflective. Membership in the Christian community is a low priority for people consumed by fast-paced, instant-access living. Becoming disciples in mission is foreign to a "me-first" cultural emphasis. What can a parish do to foster faith formation within this context?

St. James's is parish decided to face this issue head on. It had a successful formation program for children, but nothing much for adults. When they asked parishioners what they wanted, they received many good suggestions, such as Bible study, classes on parenting, conflict-management skills and explanations of Church teachings. When these were offered, however, only a few showed up. The vast majority of parishioners were untouched by these efforts.

The coordinating group whose focus was religious formation began to ask themselves, "When were parishioners touched by this parish?" The answer was obvious, although it had eluded them until now. Besides the weekend Masses, people were most often touched by special events, such as weddings, funerals, baptisms, First Communions, confirmations, being helped when in a crisis or visited when sick. It was in these moments of transition that people were touched by the parish. Might these, and others like them, be moments of faith formation as well?

The coordinating group decided to concentrate on these moments of transition that captured people's attention, times when they were open to learning and new growth. The group called together all those involved in religious education and formation. They presented their plan to see what the reaction might be. The presenters assured the assembled educators that the parish would continue to offer the traditional programs of religious formation and youth ministry. But so much more was needed to foster lifelong learning. Here was one way this could be done.

They began their presentation by asking the parish educators to consider the movement of a child from grade school into high school. This is a traumatic time for both student and parent, especially since there is more than one high school serving the area. Loyalties and friendships are in jeopardy. What opportunities for growth exist in this transition? What formational helps for both student and parent could the parish provide? This might be an excellent moment to foster clear and frank discussions between parents and children as the son or daughter moves into adolescence, along with all the struggles and difficulties this entails. The emphasis would be on small group "rap sessions" for the students themselves, as well as for parents and youth together. Some careful planning and positive image building would have to go into these sessions so that students would find them "cool" and an experience not to be missed.

Perhaps a more difficult transition is from high school to college or skill training. Preparation for college, in the present culture, begins early in high school and lasts until graduation, as students and parents travel to prospective schools, trying to decide which one is the best choice. The parish could be part of this, acting as a resource and guide. It could also locate parishioners who are either now attending or once did attend the schools being investigated and put them in contact with prospective students and parents. Once the students go off to college, care packages could be sent to all freshmen and e-mail connections made on a regular basis. The message is, "You are still part of us. We care how you are doing." What is formative about this transition is the effort by the parish to help those away from home establish links with the Church and to put them in touch with liturgies and a worshiping community in the college setting that fits their needs and desires.

As people graduate from college and begin job hunting and finding a mate, the parish needs to remain in contact with these people as a help and support during this transition. "As we operate now at St. James," one committee person said, "these people drop into a black hole, only to emerge when they come seeking marriage arrangements or baptism for their children. They need to be kept on the active parish list, mailed bulletins and newsletters, and invited to participate in activities when in the area." This is a formative time for young adults. The surrounding culture pushes them to succeed, to concentrate on making money and moving up the economic ladder, to become consumed in achieving personal goals. The parish could offer an alternative and a respite from this hectic pace. Options might include a weekend retreat following graduation, suggestions for prayer, spiritual reflection and meditation on the Internet, a trip to Central or South America as part of a two-week work camp. "There is more to life," these options say, "than making money, comfortable living and getting ahead."

The next transition that needs special attention is marriage. The ritual starts at least a year in advance as arrangements are made for the reception, the music, the entourage, the dress. It often seems as though the Church ceremony is the least important. St. James does well in offering Pre-Cana conferences and preparation materials, but could more be done to provide faith formation for the couple and family? How can we bring the parish to the people in this situation, rather than the people to the parish? It is a time filled with joy and anticipation, but also struggles and conflicts, for both those getting married and the parents. There are constant pressures to make this the most perfect day of their lives. This, of course, is an impossible objective. One option provided by the parish might be to offer mentors to the families involved, people who would visit them during the preparation, help them plan the wedding and stay in touch afterwards. Another option would be small groups for marriage couples both before and after the ceremony. This could be the occasion for them to talk about the experience with one another. Another possibility would be to use the parish website as a checklist for "getting married," not only with ideas for the ceremony, but other tips and insights as well. All of these suggestions are ways in which the parish could be part of the year-long ritual, rather than relegated to a few hours of ceremony in the midst of a hectic schedule.

Then comes children. A newborn can be a bundle of joy but it can also be a time of anxiety, disrupted lifestyles and marital stress. Rather than requiring new parents to attend pre-baptism classes to learn about the sacrament and their responsibilities, what if the parish provided a resource to parents well before the birth that included mentoring, formation and support? Just as prospective parents attend birthing classes, why not seek out pregnant couples and invite them to a formational birthing course in the parish? What an occasion for growth and new insight this could be. Rather than waiting until someone comes to church seeking baptism for their child, go to them and offer a mentoring couple experienced in parenting to listen to their concerns and provide understanding, acceptance and advice, both before and after the birth. Provide sharing sessions for those with young children, along with free baby-sitting. Sponsor "days at the park" for parents to talk with one another as they watch their children play. This is a vulnerable period for mother and father. It has great potential for spiritual growth and faith formation so long as it fits the needs and desires of each couple or single parent. The parish could do a great service by tailoring assistance and formation for these new parents.

Another transition that might be a formative moment is the empty-nest syndrome and the beginning of retirement. What outlets could the parish offer couples who have experience, energy and expertise? What occasions for growth could the parish provide as opportunities for new learning that were not possible while raising children or working full time? These newly retired people are the most likely candidates for mentoring others. For those who choose to be mentors, it would require some training and orientation. This in itself would be an excellent occasion for faith formation. Others might be willing to join service projects or volunteer programs, or be part of small group discussions. They will need, however, a personal invitation to join and positive reinforcement to remain involved.

Finally, death. Where the act of dying is not sudden but is predicted over an extended period because of terminal illness, the parish could foster occasions for families to gather around the person who is dying, helping them say goodbye and to grow in their faith. Once the person has died, the parish, which already has an excellent process of wake, funeral, burial and luncheon, could use this as a formational moment as well. This is the time friends and relatives gather to pay respects, tell stories, pray for the deceased and reflect on their own lives. What a unique opportunity for growth in one's experience of God in their lives. Special attention to death and dying in a faith context should be included as part of the entire process. Materials and books could be made available for reflection by those who are dying and those left behind. The time before the death, unless it is unexpected, could be a time for spiritual renewal of the entire family. Parishioners should be encouraged to contact the parish when someone has a terminal illness. A pastoral-care person, one of a team of trained volunteers, could be assigned to the family, to visit, bring Communion, pray with the family and encourage conversation about real and lasting values and faith issues. When the person dies, this parish Contact person helps the family prepare the funeral and stands by them throughout the ritual. There is also regular follow-ups with the family after the funeral to help with the grieving and separation process. The family is informed about all that the parish offers to help people with transitions so they can make better use of its services.

In making this proposal to the parish educators, both leaders and volunteers, the coordinating group stressed that these transitions were not the only occasions for growth and learning in the parish. Much faith formation, for instance, happens at the Masses, as well as during preparation for first sacraments and in the religious education classes. What this proposal offers is a utilization of those special moments and events in people's lives when they are more open to learning about their faith. They are less sure of themselves during transitions and are often looking for support and growth from others. What is offered is a framework for further elaboration. If adopted, it will need detailed planning for each transition, as well as organizers and volunteers to make it work, plus a budget to see it through. Should we give it a try?

After further clarification of the proposal and some lengthy discussion, St. James's staff, leaders and volunteers decided to try it for one year, at which time a careful evaluation would be made to see how well people were responding and what they had learned about their faith. The educators gave their affirmation because they knew something fresh and new was needed. People were not attending what was now being offered. It did not fit their fast-paced, hectic lifestyles. Just the newness alone could be a drawing card because of the attraction people would feel toward something never before attempted in the parish.

Planning groups were set up for each transition; eighth grade, twelfth grade, college graduates, marriage, new parenting, retirement and bereavement. This meant letting go of some of the current programs for adults. Other activities, such as small groups, could be blended into this new approach. Once the details were worked out, a presentation was made at all the Masses, followed by a town-hall meeting as a way to elicite people's reactions and input. Parishioners liked the slogan, "Bringing the Parish Into Our Lives." The response was gratifying. People signed up to be included in the pilot phase of the proposal, identifying which of the transition periods they were in at the moment and how they felt the parish might be of some assistance and support.

Does this approach satisfy the bishops' goals for adult formation of ongoing conversion, membership in the Christian community and becoming disciples on mission? Yes, if one considers that conversion comes as part of living, especially as people deal with crises and difficulties in their lives. Bonding with a community happens when people realize they cannot survive on their own and that something is missing in their lives as they get caught up in their own agenda and preoccupations. Calling people to a mission in life occurs when they discover the value and joy of working through triumphs and tragedies together. This is what lifelong learning and faith formation teaches us. The parish can be the instrument for challenging people to go deeper and discover values that are lasting.

Reaching Out in Service

One of the bishops' goals for adult faith formation is to call and prepare people to act as disciples in mission to the world. This is difficult for Americans consumed with work, family and leisure. Membership in service organizations, such as Kiwanis and Rotary Clubs, is down. Contributions to charitable causes are up but personal involvement in service projects is not.

Some causes capture people's imaginations and are well supported. One parish, for instance, established a link with a poor parish in Haiti. A few parishioners went to this country to make the initial contact. The Haitian pastor then made a personal visit to the parish. The outpouring of contributions and gifts was immediate. Truckloads of food, medicines, clothes and necessities were sent to the sister parish. Groups of parishioners went to

Haiti to help with work projects. Personal contacts were established between the two parishes.

This was a good effort that raised awareness and provided an outlet for people's generosity, but it did not flow over into the surrounding neighborhood. Although there were many people in need closer to home, these did not receive the same attention and assistance because they did not share the same mystique or glamour as did the Haitian parishioners. In order for a parish to have a service mentality that is broad based and not focused in just one area, it must have the following ingredients.

The first ingredient is that the pastor must have a well-developed social consciousness. In a parish with a dual leadership of pastor and administrator, suggested in chapter one, it helps if both leaders share this desire and thirst for social justice and care for the poor. The pastor provides the spiritual dimension and the administrator the financial and organizational backing. The two reinforce and challenge each other in this service mentality.

Given this emphasis and openness by the leadership, the next step is staff support and facilitation. The mind-set among staff must be that the parish is not here just to serve its own membership. It is here to challenge current social structures and to call people to look out for the forgotten, the helpless and the disadvantaged people in the area and in the world at large. The staff sets up a framework and provides the occasions for parishioners to interact with the poor and to discover firsthand the trials poverty brings. This works best if one staff member has this social outreach responsibility, with the support and encouragement of the staff as a whole. Examples of direct involvement include Habitat for Humanity, soup kitchens, thrift shops, overnight shelters. This direct association with poverty leads to questions about social structures in general. How is it possible, for instance, in this time of prosperity, that people still go to bed hungry? Does our thirst for consumer goods create sweatshops and child labor abuses in foreign countries? Does the expanding global economy concentrate the wealth in the hands of a few, leaving the majority still in poverty?

What the parish can provide is a concrete and direct experience of those who lack the advantages enjoyed by the majority of the parishioners. This concrete experience needs discussion before and after the encounter with those in need in order to raise the volunteers' awareness and consciousness. It also needs clear and frequent communication to the parish community by those involved in service ministry so that all know what is happening in this area.

Consider St. Gertrude's parish that just received a new pastor. Even before he arrived, it was a lively, up-to-date parish with many excellent programs and well-organized ministries. The parish was located in a well-established suburb, insulated from the cares and worries of the disadvantaged. Some outreach to the poor was being done by the social-awareness committee, but it involved only a few volunteers. Their efforts went largely unnoticed and unsupported by the parishioners. The pastor wanted to change all this.

With the help of the staff and liturgy committee, he initiated a special collection at every weekend Mass. Children brought up food and donations at the offertory, each one getting a hug from the presider. Volunteers transported these donations to a local food bank. This was well publicized so that everyone knew what happened to their contributions. Many were surprised that such an agency existed so close to home.

Next he asked the social-concerns committee to expand its membership and start dreaming of new ways to reach out to those in the surrounding neighborhood and town that needed help. "Find out where they are," he asked, "and what they need." It did not take much investigating to discover a plethora of groups and individuals needing assistance, both old and young. Local hospitals and clinics put them in touch with "charity cases." The police department gave them a list of people they had been helping. Social agencies provided many opportunities for involvement.

The committee gave a report to the staff and pastoral council. The response was, "Tell the parishioners what you have found. Put it in the bulletin. Give a report at all the Masses. People need to know about all this!" This they did and this in turn led to a new awareness by the parishioners. "The poor are right here in our midst. What should we do to help them?" "Form friendships, bond with them," was the outreach committee's response. "Contributing money and food is one thing. Getting to know them is even better. Come with us on our trips to the needy and you will discover, as we did, that *we* are the ones in need."

The pastor, as a way of raising awareness and social consciousness, asked that for the next three months every meeting in the parish begin with the phrase, "How can the needs of the poor be included in what we do at this meeting?" Each meeting was to conclude with an attempt to answer this question. People were amazed what creative responses surfaced. At a gathering of catechists who were meeting to plan next year's schedule, people suggested including service projects as part of the curriculum. "Have one evening of instruction each month concentrate on outreach and service rather than on class projects and book learning," one catechist remarked. At a liturgy meeting to plan Holy Week services, one person suggested inviting people served by the outreach ministry to come have their feet washed on Holy Thursday if they would be open to this. A new awareness, along with creative ideas, was beginning to surface among the parishioners.

People were sent out from the Masses with a mandate to pay close attention to those in need throughout the week. "Where are the poor and needy and how can we help them?" They were asked to bring back their observations and insights and drop them in the collection basket each week. Pencils and cards were placed in the pews for this purpose. The new tradition of children bringing up donations at the offertory was catching on. New and bigger containers had to be placed around the altar for all the food and money collected. The outreach committee established many new sub-committees, each one directing a different task or project. Notices in the bulletin and announcements at Mass brought these projects to the attention of the parishioners and provided an outlet for their involvement. Parish-wide "Festivals For Justice" were held twice a year. One was in the summer as a kickoff for a large contingent of parishioners, ages sixteen to seventy, traveling to a parish in need, usually in another country, as part of a work-camp project. The other was in December as parishioners prepared food baskets and toys for families in need so they could have a happy Christmas.

All this concrete and direct involvement prepared the way for the parish challenging unjust structures in society. One outreach project was visiting the prison in a nearby town. This was a new experience for parishioners. Little was being done in the prison to provide for rehabilitation. The volunteers got permission to set up a computer lab in the prison. Using donated computers, they began to teach the prisoners skills for using the Internet and designing websites. This would provide a good living when they were released from prison and some promise of escaping the circle of poverty that put them in prison in the first place. The computers also made it possible for prisoners to link up with a "pen pal" from the parish via e-mail. This got people thinking and talking about the death penalty. Some of the injustices of the system began to emerge, including poor representation by counsel and unreliable evidence in trials. This led to a movement by parishioners to question the death penalty and to contact their legislators for a moratorium on capital punishment and a reassessment of the penal system.

Without fanfare and with little resistance, the parish was changing into a community of service. Contributions had risen ever since it was announced that ten percent of the offertory collection would go to worthy causes. Teens were signing up months in advance to be part of the work project abroad. It had become the "cool" thing to do each summer. Parishioners no longer contributed only money to charitable causes. They were showing up to help out in person. Children were learning the joy of giving at the weekend Masses as they returned to their seats full of smiles from bringing up their food items. The outreach committee was elated that their initial efforts at uncovering local needs had created such a groundswell in the parish. The pastor and administrator were giving each other winks for all that had taken place in such a short time. "Changing the image will change behaviors," was their motto. The service orientation of the parish now had a life of its own. No longer did it depend on the pastor's or the administrator's input and initiative. There was interaction among groups in the parish. Parishioners had discovered for themselves the joy of these new connections. Those being helped were just like themselves, with names and faces and smiles which came to the fore when they were loved and accepted for who they are, God's own children in bewildering beauty and diversity.

Connecting with the Fringe

Evangelization is a desire for both staffs and leaders but it is still a lost art in parishes. Connecting with those on the fringe, the inactive, uninvolved and disinterested parishioners, is touted as a priority but it receives little attention and hardly any share of the budget. Yet this is where the *majority* of Catholics reside, on the fringes of the Church and parish life. Less than half of those registered in a parish now attend Mass on a regular basis, send their children to religious formation or contribute financially. Taking the parish to the people means connecting with this large mass of Catholics on the edges of the Church.

Jeremy Langford wrote an article in the April 22, 2000, issue of *America* entitled "Ministering to Gen-X Catholics, Jesus Style." Although it was directed to young-adults ministry, it could be used as a method for reaching all those on the fringe, young and old alike. He describes his own conversion experience as the result of a parish community reaching out to him. "It was not until I found a community of fellow seekers in an exciting parish that I felt energized enough by Catholicism to explore its riches." He goes on to suggest the story of Jesus' walk with the two disciples to Emmaus as a good model of evangelization. It includes the actions of "walking with," "listening to," "talking with," "breaking bread with" and "empowering."

The first step is to go to those on the fringe and listen to what they are saying. Just walk with them and listen. That is enough, at least in the beginning. Pay attention to their needs, cares, concerns, joys, sorrows and difficulties. Put yourself in their shoes. That is what makes Oprah Winfrey's program so popular. She listens and accepts people as they are, both gifted and spiritual, flawed and needy. This is what Jesus did. "What were you talking about on your walk?" he said to those on the way to Emmaus (Luke 24:17). How would that play out in a modern parish setting?

St. Francis parish decided to change its focus from the people coming to church to those who don't. The pastor announced this at all the Masses. "From now on," he said, "the *real* Church is out there in the lives of the people who are not here." The people in the pews looked at one another and wondered what was coming next. They knew something was brewing. The pastor had been hinting at this for weeks. "Our task," he went on, "is to locate these people and discover Church in their midst. I need your help. You know who these people are, your own family members, relatives and friends. We have names of people on our parish lists that do not come to church, but I suspect there are many others besides these people. How can we reach them? And once we do, what do we say to them? Got any ideas? In the pews are some cards and pencils. Write down anyone you think we should contact or any ideas you have about what we should say once we do make contact. Put the cards in the collection basket. After Mass, as part of our coffee and donuts, I will fill you in a little more about all this and then we can discuss it."

The curious came down for coffee, wondering what this was all about. What they learned was that the pastoral council had chosen as the parish theme for the coming year, "The People Are the Church—Go Find It." Every program, ministry and committee was to work on this theme for the coming year. Using Jesus' model of ministry, the theme suggested that people on the fringe were the Church. Jesus included tax collectors, prostitutes, loan sharks, fishermen, beggars, cripples, the sick and dying in his Church. This is what the parish should do as well.

First of all, those on the fringe have to be identified. Some may be registered in the parish but have stopped attending. Others may call themselves Catholic but are not members of any parish. Still others may not belong to any religion but still have the potential to "be Church." Go find out who they are.

The pastor went on to explain that the parish website would be changing to reflect this new emphasis. People would have the opportunity to express their feelings and concerns via e-mail, whether or not they were members of the parish or even lived in the area. "People could belong here," he said, "and not live in the same town, state or country. They are still Church to us."

Not only the website but also parish ministries would be changing. "In order to walk with and listen to the people on the fringe," he explained, "we will have to step out of our buildings and the comfort of our surroundings and go out to where the people are. We are not inviting them back to church, not yet, perhaps not ever. But we do want to know what they are discussing as they walk along. How can we do this?" The new parish website would include meditations and prayers for the marketplace, short scriptural quotes and reflections to help people through the day. It would also ask probing questions and challenge people's accepted way of acting, helping them identify unjust systems and unethical practices in the workplace.

The weekday Masses would be offered at different times each day, hoping to entice working people in for some spiritual nourishment. This would be a small crowd at first, but it might have a ripple effect. The pastor went on to say, "What we ask of you is to keep this new emphasis in mind and observe throughout your day what people are doing, where they go, what they watch, what stirs their hearts, what they read and talk about, and with whom. Each Sunday you will be invited to write down on the cards in the pews your observations and drop them in the collection basket. This will become part of your donation to the parish."

The pastor suggested that next fall the parish might sponsor a USF week. This stands for "University of St. Francis." Each night of the week the parish will offer courses in a wide range of subjects, including computer science, practical skills, dancing, literature and spiritual topics. "We hope that people on the fringe," the pastor said, "will teach some of these courses in computer skills, the Internet, painting, writing, investing, parenting, methods of prayer. It will be a celebration of all our gifts as a parish. So as you walk with and listen to the outsider, discover what they could offer us as a parish community."

Part of walking with and listening to the people on the fringe of Church is discovering the multi-cultural makeup of the surrounding area. "We are not all alike by any means," the pastor remarked. "Some are from Mexico, Central and South America. Some come from Asia and the Pacific Islands, as well as the Orient, Western and Eastern Europe. Seek them out, listen to the languages they speak, put yourself in their shoes and see what it feels like being an alien in a strange land. All these people are Church to us."

The people listened attentively to the pastor's words, not understanding all the implications but catching on to his enthusiasm and motivation. Almost everyone present could identify someone they knew who was Catholic but was no longer active in the Church. Perhaps they could make a contact over the next week and see what they had to say about all this.

The staff and council members were watching the reactions of the people during Mass and at the coffee session afterwards. This was a big step for the leadership. It meant a new direction and focus for them. Some of the staff's job descriptions had to be adapted to fit this new emphasis. Less time would be available for the traditional tasks of parish ministry as more time and energy was devoted to connecting with the "fringe people." This was uncharted territory and no one had any idea what it would entail. The council members were anxious to see how people, especially the active ones, would react to their theme and new direction. Would people get angry when their pet project or ministry is given less attention and money, as more emphasis is given to this new orientation? So far, the response was positive. No telling what the next few weeks and months might bring. The pastor was hoping people would catch on to the sentiments of walking with and listening to the inactive people. This was not a proselytizing effort to increase parish membership. It was to discover God at work on the fringe and in the lives of the "outsiders."

Once these people were identified and invited to speak their minds, they might start talking. Then what? Would they want a forum to express their hopes and fears, longings and disappointments? Could the parish provide that occasion without judgment or prejudice? That was the goal. Listen, enter into dialogue, establish rapport and a safe environment for them to talk. This could be face-to-face visits in homes or in small groups. It could be in cyberspace via chat rooms and e-mail. It could be in informal gatherings on church property; anywhere people would be willing to share their thoughts and feelings. That does not mean that the Gospel message would be watered down to appease and placate current lifestyles. "We speak our truth and God's love as we know it," was the pastor's hope and desire, "though not as 'lording it over others' as Jesus cautioned the disciples."

"Above all," the pastor exclaimed, "the weekend liturgies at St. Francis parish need to be welcoming, attractive and inclusive places of worship if and when these people on the fringe want to join in. Is it possible to create an environment of people enjoying one another's company and the presence of the Lord all wrapped up in one? Can we open our arms and our hearts to newcomers and those unlike ourselves?"

The pastor went on to explain that once the parish locates and listens to those on the fringe, it then needs to create special occasions that will be of interest to them. One liturgy each month could have as its theme, "Worship During Mass, Free Coffee Afterwards." Other occasions might include sharing a meal together or offering opportunities for informal conversation. "I would like to initiate a monthly 'Rap With St. Francis' on Sunday evenings," the pastor explained. "There would be a different theme for each Sunday that would be posted on the parish website and announced at the Masses. We will start right away, next week. Everyone is welcome. Be sure to bring your friends. The first theme will be, 'What makes shy people get up and do what needs to be done?' We will start with a gathering of the whole group to set the tone and then break into smaller groups for sharing. We will pass around large loaves of bread at the beginning as a way of breaking bread together. The emphasis will be on what it is like being on the outside looking in. Why is it so hard breaking into groups? When do you want to be alone and when with a group?

Can we help people feel more a part of the parish? How can we help people feel at home here? The sessions will be one hour long, start to finish. At the end, the total group will decide what the focus for the next gathering will be. Food and drink will follow."

"Meals are special," he went on to say, "but people are reluctant to invite others into their homes. The parish can certainly provide meals on church property. That is, after all, what the Eucharist is all about, a meal. But those on the fringe may not be ready or willing to show up at church. Is there a middle ground, an event that might not be so intimidating or difficult, especially if there are little children? What about a progressive dinner several times a year? It would take some organizing but it could be fun. Five families to a group, five homes to visit, no more than half an hour at each place. They might even be strangers to one another, at least at the beginning of the evening. They could drop off their children at church for baby-sitting. They would start with a topic to explore at the first stop. Then on to appetizers and drinks at the next stop. Salads at the third, followed by the main dish at the fourth place and ending with dessert at the fifth. This would amount to two hours of good eating, creative conversation and enjoyment by all, without too much of a burden to any one household." Without realizing it, the pastor was exemplifying what Jeremy Langford said in his article on Gen-Xers, "Jesus treated every meal as a sacred event. For the Emmaus disciples, the meal provided a pivotal moment; it allowed them the chances to welcome and come to know the stranger."

The intention in all this was to redirect parish energies in order to locate, walk with, listen to and break bread with the outsiders, with those on the fringe. One more step remained, that of empowerment. Is it possible to turn these people on the fringe into disciples? That is what Jesus did. He cured people and then sent them off to heal others. The woman at the well, who was certainly a person on the fringe of her society, discovered the Christ and then went running off to tell others, leaving her water jug behind. She had no need for it, her life had changed. "Come out and see the man who told me everything I have ever done. Could this be 'Christ'?" (John 4:29) Could those at St. Francis's parish empower others as Jesus did this woman?

Perhaps the parish could provide opportunities for people to help others improve the world around them. Along with a welcoming and inclusive atmosphere at the Masses and other occasions that help people interact and feel at home in the parish community, could the parish also challenge the marginal members to make a difference in their own lives? "One thing we could do," the pastor suggested, "would be to invite them to join us as we help out at the soup kitchen each month, or build houses for the poor or join us with the neighborhood cleanup each year. Another is to challenge them to maintain a reasonable workload so there is time for family and personal reflection. We could initiate discussions on ethical practices at work or socially conscious choices in their investments. This is only the tip of the iceberg. Once we open up the possibilities and present the options, the people themselves will fill in the blanks. All we need to do is get their attention, show them we care, capture their imaginations and the rest will fall into place."

This was heady stuff for the people attending the coffee and donuts after Mass. What exactly was the pastor asking of them? Go out and locate the people who don't come to church? "That is not hard," one grandparent remarked, "Most of my children do not attend Mass. I suppose I could call them and ask them what they think about the Catholic Church and this plan you are presenting. Is that what you are asking?"

"What we are trying to get across," the pastor responded, "is that those of you who do come to church regularly are the ones who must connect with those who don't. Do not start by inviting them back to church. Find out, instead, what stirs their hearts, what issues and concerns fill their lives, what turns them off about Church, how they pray or relate to God. If they want to come back, we are here for them, especially at the monthly 'free-breakfast' Mass or the Sunday evening rap sessions, or the USF week or the progressive dinner parties. They can plug into our website or call up our special 'Thought for the Day' phone line. They can send us an e-mail with suggestions or give them to you to put in the collection basket. Just remember that they are the Church as much as you and I are. Remember our theme, 'The People Are the Church—Go Find It.' That is your task. Go find the Church in the lives and families, the hearts and minds of your children and grandchildren, relatives and friends, and others like them. If Jesus did it, so can we. He promised us the Spirit to see us through this."

It is still too soon to know if this approach at St. Francis will succeed. This is a new way of being parish, and changes of this magnitude take time. So far, both leaders and parishioners are pleased by what they are witnessing. New banners are going up along the street in front of church welcoming people to attend. New and fresh ideas are appearing in the collection basket, along with names to add to the parish roster. An article appeared in the diocesan newspaper interviewing the pastor, staff and council members about this new emphasis. People from near and far are sending in e-mails inquiring about this new way of operating. Some are from other Catholic parishes asking for literature and descriptions about how they might try this same approach. The leaders find this amazing. "We haven't a clue about what we are doing," a council member quipped, "and already others are asking us how to go about it. At least the word is getting out."

Perhaps the best proof that it is working is the young woman who showed up at the first Sunday evening session. She sat in the back and was reluctant to share when the gathering broke up into small groups. Only at the end, when the entire group was trying to decide the topic for the rap session next month, did she raise her hand and say, "I'm that shy person who has to get up and do what needs to be done. I was not going to come tonight but my next-door neighbor took a chance in mentioning it and inviting me to come. This evening made an unbearable week bearable. It has given me the courage to go in Monday and quit my abusive job. I think the topic for next time should be, 'Critiquing the workplace; what should be allowed and what should not be tolerated.' I have lots to share." Everyone clapped and shouted their support and agreed that this would be the next subject for discussion. The pastor said in response, "I think I have just discovered the Church."

Forming a Covenant with the People

The focus of this chapter is to take the parish to the people, to bridge the gaps between Church and people's everyday lives. For the church-goers, this means forming bonds and relationships in ways that relate to those "on the run." For the non-reflective, urban, modernized parishioners, it means paying attention to the transitions that fill their lives and drawing upon their need for faith formation and spiritual growth during these critical moments. For the insulated, self-contained, it means capturing their attention and showing them the underbelly of the society. The parish needs to raise their awareness and make it easy for them to respond and help out in simple and concrete ways. For the dropouts and the uninvolved, it means uncovering the depth and yearning that lies beneath and providing a place where they can tell their story. For the faithful volunteers, it means not getting overwhelmed by the scope and breadth of the task that lies ahead. Others will come to fill the ranks and take their place in ministry. They will need to be invited, however, and drawn in with incremental steps of involvement. For the pastors and administrators, staffs and leaders, it means be creative. Don't settle for less. Discover the Church in the people, wherever they are. That is where the Spirit of Jesus resides.

An Example of Adult Formation
As Manifested by the Leaders and People of
St. Dominic Catholic Community, Brookfield, Wisconsin

By
Patrick J. Russell, Ph.D.
Director of Adult and Family Ministry

In order to foster a new appreciation of Bible study, St. Dominic's parish has developed a unique adult formation program called **The Parish Parable Project**. It consists of three parts:

Stage One: The Parable Seminar: By means of bulletin announcements and personal contacts, a group of parishioners gathered together to study twenty-two parables found in the Gospels. This "Parable Seminar" met every two weeks to study the parables of Jesus and learn what was at the heart of his teaching. Each participant chose one book written by a respected scholar on the parables to use as a reference. They agreed to read before each session sections of their book and fill out index cards about what they had discovered. Their research included a description of the scholar's interpretation, valuable cultural, literary and historical background material and one significant quote from the book about the parable. The technique of giving each person a different book to study meant each person came with something unique to contribute to the discussion so that everyone was on a similar footing in terms of knowledge to share. No one, in other words, had all the truth. Everyone had different pieces to contribute to the whole. It was also important that the abilities of each participant were matched with an appropriate scholarly work on the parables. Books were shifted among members after the first few meetings until they all found a book they could understand and enjoy.

Two parables were chosen for each biweekly session. The meeting began with prayer and then a "round-robin" discussion about the information each person had garnered from one's research on each parable. Once this was completed, the group then discussed how their new understanding would apply to the modern-day believer and what might be contemporary applications of these parables. The goal of the session was to craft an explanation of each parable that could guide others in walking more faithfully the way of Jesus.

Each member of the Parable Seminar selected two parables and made a commitment to produce a recorded Bible lesson on the meaning and application of those parables. When one of these parables became the subject of discussion, that person would take notes on what people discovered and how these insights might prove helpful to others. This information would be used for the next phase of the project.

Stage Two: Phone-A-Parable: After the study of all of the parables had been completed, and the recordings prepared for each one, these Bible lessons were then posted each week, from Epiphany to Pentecost, on the parish phone system and on the parish website. Parishioners were encouraged, through various publicity efforts, to call the parish and listen to these weekly Phone-A-Parable messages.

What made this second stage successful was the work and dedication of the original study group. The participants were faithful in preparing the material and attending each session so that informative and reflective recorded Bible lessons could be constructed. The effort at producing recorded telephone messages for the entire parish community gave their individual study and group discussions a sense of purpose and urgency. They began to realize that the personal gathering of information and the shared insights from the discussions were not just for their own personal growth but for the parish community as well.

The seminar on parables was seen as a pebble thrown into a pond. The recorded "Phone-A-Parable" messages were cast out into the parish community to see what effect they would have on others. The phone number with the parable message was publicized in the bulletin, through announcements at Mass, posters on parish property, school flyers, the archdiocesan newspaper, the parish website, even listed on refrigerator magnets given out to parishioners.

The caller was offered four options after dialing the parable phone line: listen to that week's parable lesson, listen to the previous week's lesson, hear a description of the Parable Seminar and its process leading to the recorded messages, or record one's own thoughts and reflections after listening to the parable lesson. The text of each week's lesson was also posted on the parish website, along with an annotated bibliography of the books used in preparation for the recorded lesson.

Stage Three: Parish Discussion Groups: In addition to being able to listen and respond to the recorded parable lessons, parishioners were also able to join discussion groups during Lent. Many of these groups were organized around particular vocations and interests, including one's profession, family status or state in life. The small groups used the recorded Phone-A-Parable messages as the basis for their Bible study and faith sharing during their weekly meetings.

Each discussion group was supplied with a CD and an audiotape that contained each parable lesson, as well as additional materials geared toward fostering a lively discussion on the meaning of each parable and its application toward living an authentic life of faith. Each discussion group had a trained facilitator who called the group together and provided direction.

The Parish Parable Project was just one small pebble in the life of the parish and its people. Jesus did say that the Kingdom of God was like the smallest of seeds. The strength of this project was that it manifested a fundamental truth about adult formation: Learning about life's meaning is a communitarian endeavor, not something to be done on one's own. This Bible study process was structured in a community setting through the Parable Seminar and its extension to the larger parish was likewise communitarian. The seminar group members that studied the parables were not learning just for themselves but were providing a service to the entire parish. By empowering these people with this responsibility and making them the voices of instruction through the phone messages, it showed in a tangible way that each believer is called through baptism to teach others and to witness to their faith. All are called to be priests, prophets and leaders, that is, to be *ministers* of the divine presence rippling wonderfully and mysteriously throughout our human experience.

(St. Dominic Catholic Community is located at 18255 W. Capital Drive, Brookfield, Wisconsin 53045. The phone number is 262-781-3480. Their e-mail address is parish@stdominic.net)

CHAPTER SEVEN

MANAGING THE PARISH:
THE PRACTICAL SIDE OF THE COVENANT

I will maintain my covenant with you
and your descendants after you
throughout the ages as an everlasting pact,
to be your God and the God of your descendants after you . . .

On your part, you and your descendants after you
must keep my covenant throughout the ages.
—GENESIS 17:7, 9

The theme of this book is that a change of system for Catholic parishes needs to take place. A system that requires co-leaders for all ministries, including the management of the parish, may be a better way of operating. The pastor would be the spiritual and sacramental leader, while the administrator or some other staff person would manage the temporal affairs.

This second leader could be hired by the pastor, the pastoral council or an administration committee. The person could also be appointed by the diocese. Roger Gambatese proposed this in a letter to the editor (*America*, July 1-8, 2000, p. 30): "A good place to start would be for the bishops to take away from the pastor the responsibility to manage the parish and place the responsibility instead on a lay person appointed by and accountable to the bishop, not the pastor. Parish managers would be trained and supervised by the bishop's office. . . . I am confident that in almost every parish there are lay people with management expertise that equals or exceeds the management expertise of the pastor. . . . To protect the pastor from parishioners' complaints about parish management, bishops must make it clear to all that the role of the pastor and other priests assigned to the parish shall be that of administering the sacraments, teaching the message of the Gospels, and counseling parishioners, and that the pastor is not responsible for, and has no accountability for, managing the parish" (Re: "Are We Killing Our Priests?" April 20, 2000).

This day has not yet come, but it is worth pursuing. Divide up the responsibilities between pastor and one other person who is a co-leader with the pastor. Choosing that person is critical because the job demands a knowledge of how the Church and the parish operate, as well as having well-developed management skills. One parish I encountered had this arrangement of pastor and administrator. They were equal partners as co-leaders of the parish. One reason it worked so well is because the pastor was willing to let go of the temporal, personnel and financial reins of the parish. The administrator was savvy about how the parish system worked and was confident in his own abilities to direct the temporal affairs with authority, humor and grace. It helped that the administrator was an inactive priest, well gifted in organizational skills. Because this position is new and largely untested, this chapter will explore the scope and role of this co-equal administrative leader of the parish.

Making the Right Choice

Holy Redeemer is a medium-sized parish on the outskirts of the city. It has a staff of six, including the principal of the parish school, a director of religious education, a youth minister, the liturgy/music minister and a pastoral associate who directs the outreach ministries, plus, of course, the pastor. The neighboring parish will soon be without a pastor. Rather than closing it down, the bishop and the diocesan planning office decided to appoint a pastoral administrator and asked the pastor of Holy Redeemer to be the sacramental minister of the parish. This would mean that he would be presiding at the Masses and handling sacramental duties of the neighboring parish while continuing all his current responsibilities at Holy Redeemer. While seeing the wisdom of the plan, he felt cornered by the move. How could he cope with this extra assignment? His plate was already full.

As soon as he found out the news, he called a joint session of pastoral council and staff. He laid out the situation. "I will not be able to handle all my duties, " he said. "Something has to give. What would you think if we hired a parish administrator to run Holy Redeemer? I would, of course, still be the pastor. But this new person would share equally in the leadership of the parish with the responsibility of coordinating the staff, administering the temporal affairs, overseeing the finances and managing parish operations. This would mean a significant shift for us all. There would be, in effect, two 'bosses,' one for the spiritual side and one for the temporal side. Could you handle this? Could the parishioners handle it? Can *I* handle it? Only time will tell. But it is better than what I see the present reality to be—a strung out, overworked, inefficient pastor and a floundering parish as a result. What do you think?"

The rest of the meeting was filled with questions and concerns, as scenarios about how this might work out at Holy Redeemer circulated around the room. A staff member asked the pastor, "Do you mean that the one in charge of the staff would no longer be yourself?" "That's right. I would be one member along with the rest of you on staff. It would be facilitated by the administrator. That is why we have to be sure to get someone with whom we can all work and feel at ease." A council member asked, "Can we afford such a person? This position will not come cheaply." The pastor replied, "Can we afford *not* to? My hospital bills when I collapse from exhaustion would be much more expensive."

At the end of the conversation, the staff and council decided to bring this to a gathering of the parishioners and get their reactions. The people were informed that this would not be a vote by the parish. The pastor, staff and council would have to come to a consensus as a group if it were to happen. But the people needed to be asked their opinion. The town-hall meeting scheduled after the last Mass on Sunday morning had two hundred people in attendance. This was an excellent manifestation of interest and concern. The pastor presented to the gathering the same proposal he submitted to the staff and council. The assembly then broke into smaller groups of eight to ten people, each one facilitated by a staff or council member. The task of the small groups was to answer the question, "Do we or don't we hire an administrator as co-leader of the parish?"

The result of the town hall, as announced at all the Masses the next weekend, was to give it a try. Not everyone agreed. Many didn't like sharing the pastor with another parish. Most, however, saw the wisdom of the plan and gave it their support and affirmation, at least for the coming year. In response, the pastor asked the people to contribute five to ten percent more than they now gave as a way of supporting this new adventure. "I am convinced," he said at the Masses, "that this position will lead to a better parish community. Your added donations will be put to good use."

The staff and council finalized the decision and the difficult task of finding the right person began. Ads were placed in local, diocesan and national publications. A job description was drawn up and a search committee formed. Many people submitted resumes, both from within and outside the parish. Eventually one person was chosen, a surprise candidate who lived across town. Ann Savage had unique qualifications, was active in her parish and familiar with Church politics and structures. In her youth she had been a Jesuit volunteer for a few years and, in her words, "I have never been the same since." Her father owned a local bank and when he retired, she took over. She was well organized, knew how to get the most out of people and was an easy person to work with. The bank thrived under her direction, but independent banks were becoming a relic of the past. She saw the writing on the wall, sold the bank and began looking for a new challenge in life. Her three children were either in college or starting families of their own. Along came the ad from Holy Redeemer. She submitted an application and was chosen as the best person for the job.

That all happened a year and a half ago. She took over in September, encountering some apprehension from leaders and people, along with a smattering of latent hostility. That is all in the past now. The staff, leaders, parishioners, and especially the pastor, all praise her efforts and are amazed at what she has accomplished in such a short time. What follows is the story of that year and a half.

Starting with Staff

From the very first meeting with the staff, Ann felt included as one of them and accepted as their leader. The pastor made this possible. He was so relieved to have someone else run the meetings and manage all that had to be accomplished. His gift had never been organizational skills, and previous staff meetings had deteriorated into reporting sessions. No longer.

Ann inaugurated a new way of interacting and functioning as a staff. She asked staff members to come prepared with quality agenda items that included not only information sharing but planning items as well. These were issues that the staff could work on as a whole. She also asked them to bring along feedback items, both positive and negative, that might improve the level of ministry among staff members and in the parish as a whole. A new atmosphere of energy and anticipation accompanied the meetings. The hour-and-a-half sessions on Wednesday mornings were no longer a chore. Attendance improved. Even the principal found a way of being present, discovering two volunteers who could fill in at the school office during her absence. Ann did not lead all the staff meetings but rather suggested this be done on a rotating basis. She did, however, meet briefly before and after each meeting with the leader to make sure the person felt comfortable with the task and was doing a good job.

Soon lunch was added to the end of the staff meetings. People were enjoying one another's company more and wanted to stay together longer. The lunches became occasions for celebrating birthdays and anniversaries, as well as acknowledging personal achievements. In one of the daily "run-throughs" between Ann and the pastor, she confided that it was her experience at the bank that if the staff enjoyed one another's company, everything else would take care of itself. "The more we can all work as a team," she told him, "the happier everyone will be. This will manifest itself in the way they do their tasks." "That is what I had always hoped would happen," the pastor remarked, "but I never knew how to go about it."

Ann made a point of visiting every staff person's ministry so she could get acquainted with the scope and challenges of the person's job. Staff members appreciated her presence and interest in their work, which gave them a sense of self-worth and provided them with the chance to show off their skills and insights. She also inaugurated an overnight for the staff twice a year, one in the fall to set up the year's schedule and one in the spring to evaluate how well they had done. The overnights became occasions for both work and play. Her wit and humor were infectious. The pastor had to admit he never experienced so much laughter and fun among a staff in all the years he had been ordained.

Once the staff was up and running, the next area to tackle was the management of the parish as a whole. Ann approached it from four different vantage points, all connected and dependent on each other. The first area was to refine parish structures and establish a strategic plan for the parish. Where could it be in three to five years and how would it get there? The other three areas included managing the human potential of the parish, dealing with the politics and improving the parish's image.

Creating a Plan

Ann began with the pastoral council, asking its members to review the parish mission statement to make sure it described the core values and purpose of the parish. "Does it," she asked, "describe who we are as a parish, what is our function, how we achieve our purpose and for whom?" Over the next month, council members reflected on the statement individually, did some background reading and came to the next council meeting prepared to either keep the same statement or revise it. The consensus among the members was that it was time to revise the mission statement. Over the next two hours, a new one was crafted that summed up the essentials of Holy Redeemer. It read:

> We, the Holy Redeemer parish community, believe we are called, as a Eucharistic People, to live the Gospel values of Jesus Christ within the Roman Catholic tradition. We seek to be a welcoming, inclusive community, responding compassionately to the needs of others, through a prayerful discernment of the gifts and resources of our people.

The council was proud of its work, displaying the new statement in the back of church, in the bulletin, as take-home cards in the pews and on the parish website. Over the next month people had a chance to give their reactions, offer suggestions and corrections and indicated how it described their own experience of the parish. Once it was finalized, the pastor used it in place of the Creed at all the weekend Masses. "This is who we are as a parish," he said. "This is our Belief Statement as a community."

With a revised mission statement in hand, the next step was to call a full-day meeting of all leadership groups in order to construct a strategic plan for the next three to five years. "We know *who* we are as a parish," Ann said by way of introduction. "Now we need to know *where* we are going in liturgy, in forming community, in formation, in outreach and in administration." Each area of ministry worked on its own to construct two or three goals for the next few years. The groups reassembled to critique and refine each other's goals and then chose one goal in each area to work on for the rest of the meeting. People returned to their ministry groups and constructed action plans that would help each group come closer to realizing one of its goals. By the end of the day, each area of ministry had goals to work on and concrete action steps for achieving at least one of the goals. The pastor came over at the end of the session and bursting with enthusiasm, told Ann, "You are amazing! No wonder your bank did so well. You really know how to get the most out of people, without even pushing them. Look at these people. They worked hard all day long and they still are full of smiles, happy to have accomplished so much for the present and future life of the parish." Her response to the pastor was, "I have only accomplished a fourth of my job as the parish administrator. Yes, we now have a plan of action which looks great on paper. Getting it accomplished is another thing entirely. So far all we have done is managed the structures of the parish. We have yet to manage the human resources. That is our next task, you and I. I can't do it alone. You will have to do it with me."

Uncovering the Potential

The next area Ann Savage tackled was to tap into the vast reservoir of talent and goodwill that lay hidden in the parish. Up to this point, whenever a job needed to get done, those in charge went out looking for volunteers. They usually found people they knew, those already involved in other parish functions and ministries. Ann recognized that this was not the most efficient and productive way to operate. She called together the stewardship committee and asked the members how they went about the time/talent side of their ministry. "We have a sign-up weekend each year," they explained, "but it is always the same people who volunteer. We need some new ideas and hope you can help us out." "I'll try," she replied, "or rather *we'll* try and together we will find inspiration."

Her first suggestion was to make up a one-sheet standardized form that the committee would give to every group and ministry in the parish. The sheet was to help uncover the needs these groups had for volunteers. The instructions indicated that the name and description of the task went on the sheet, along with the time required to do it, the training or background necessary, the number of meetings people have to attend and the contact persons to call if interested. It also included a place for people to sign up for the task. Once that was done, the committee sponsored a parish-wide Ministry Fair to display all the groups and ministries that existed in the parish. This was followed by a Commitment Weekend during which people were encouraged to fill out the volunteer sheets. Once the sheets were returned, leaders in each area followed up on the responses, making sure volunteers were contacted within two weeks of their commitment. The stewardship committee monitored the process, making sure that those signing up for a task were pleased with what they chose. The committee also made sure those in charge of ministries provided the training and support necessary for people to feel wanted and confident in their new task. This coordination of volunteers was the first step in uncovering the human potential of the parish.

The second step was making direct contact with those who had not made a commitment. Ann was convinced that most parishioners were not against volunteering, they just needed to be asked. She formed a select committee of telephoners who had only one task: to call ten people every other week and ask people if they would be willing to help out in the parish. They made the calls from the parish office during evening hours. They had access to the parish computers that showed what jobs were still open and thus needed more volunteers. In making the calls, they scrolled through the jobs on the computer until the person they were calling found one that looked appealing. The telephoner made note of this and promised a follow-up call by someone in that ministry within the next two weeks. The person was assured there would be no pressure, just an invitation to get involved. The positive response to this personal invitation was beyond anyone's expectation. On average, six of the ten people called said they would like to get involved. They had never been asked before, nor did they realize all the possible options that existed. The remaining four people telephoned, men and women, were not resistant. They just did not feel they had the time to volunteer right now. Almost to a person they asked that the parish give them another call in six months. Perhaps by then they would be able to work a parish ministry into their schedule. The callers also received many unsolicited comments about the parish, mostly positive in nature. As one person remarked, "I don't know what is going on at Holy Redeemer these days. I come to Mass but to nothing else, and I must say I have sensed a new spirit recently. People seem happier and are enjoying themselves more. This includes the pastor as well. Keep up the good work." The six people on the telephoning committee found their task most rewarding. Not only did they uncover new people as volunteers, they were also able to provide feedback to the staff and council about what people thought about the parish. The pastor was delighted with the outcome. It provided concrete, relevant material for his homilies, and affirmed the choice of Ann being the right person for the administrator's job. In telling her this, Ann laughed and said, "We are still only halfway there. The management of structures and volunteers has gone well. Now on to politics and image."

Coping with Politics

It was not long after Ann took the administrator's job that she heard rumblings about "this upstart who thinks she is the pastor." She let it ride, knowing that this new way of operating would be an adjustment for all. She hoped that over time the rumors and resistance would die out. That was largely true, but one cadre of "old timers" dug in its heels. "The pastor is the sole boss of the parish," someone heard them say. "What right does someone else, a woman no less, have to make decisions and set directions?" No amount of explanation and support by the pastor made a difference. Their minds were made up, so much so that they initiated a letter-writing campaign to the bishop to have this "experiment," as they put it, stopped at once. When the pastor showed Ann the letters sent to him from the chancery, she laughed and said, "I had been expecting this." "Then you have a plan?" the pastor said in amazement. His approach to such conflicts had always been to ignore them and hope they would disappear. "Sure," she said. "Hit it head on." Which she did.

The letters were not signed, but everyone knew those behind it: a few stalwarts of the Senior's Club who felt slighted when the pastor no longer came to their meetings. He had to drop such events when he took on the new duties at the neighboring parish. Ann showed up at their next meeting and, in a most disarming manner, asked to be put on the agenda. She caught them by surprise. She knew that in managing parish politics, the rule of thumb is to speak to their self-interests. "Let me start off," she said, "by handing out some index cards and pencils. These are just blank cards. I need your help. On one side, write down one thing that disturbs you about my being the administrator of this parish. On the other side, write down one thing you like about the pastor." That was a surprise but they settled down to writing on the cards. Once this was done, she asked them to share what was on the cards with the person next to them. This they did, wondering what the next step might be. "All right," she said, "let's make a list of all the things you like about the pastor." She wrote their comments on a flip chart, filling up two large pieces of paper. "Now what would be your reaction if he had to leave because of ill health? That is what he said would happen if he did not have an administrator to help out in the parish. Given that reality, how can I help you deal with what disturbs you about my being here? I am here so that your pastor can remain healthy. How can we make a go of it, you and I?" After a few moments of silence, one woman raised her hand and said, "How can we get our pastor to come to our meetings again?" "That's easy," Ann responded. "Have your monthly meetings on Tuesdays instead of Mondays. I can promise you he will be here, at least for a few minutes at the beginning of your meetings." "We can do that." "Then you have a deal." This, of course, had all been worked out ahead of time with the pastor. He was amazed at how easily she had handled the situation. "It just takes a little bargaining and a great deal of 'moxie.' They have to know what they are dealing with here. I had a much harder time with the all-male board of directors I inherited from my father at the bank. Now the next area of politics is the finances. That won't be so easy."

Although the pastor had requested a five- to ten-percent increase in contributions to pay for the new administrator, the income level was still far below what it should be for a parish the size of Holy Redeemer. The pastor had never mentioned money from the pulpit and the stewardship committee had not been direct enough in seeking increases to people's financial contributions. As a result, only about a quarter of the membership was using envelopes and the average donation was only about one percent of a person's income.

Ann set up a combined meeting of the stewardship committee and the finance council, asking them to work out a plan together. "We need to get people's attention," she said. "I know from my time at the bank that there is a vast, untapped reservoir of money if we can only discover ways to help people invest in the parish. That is what it is, an investment. Take wills and stocks, for instance. We need to make it simple and easy for people to make bequeaths and donate stock options to the parish. Passing a basket is an outdated mode of contributing. Everything else in people's lives is made by automatic payment, credit cards or via the Internet. Why not the parish?" This got the committee and council members' attention. But they responded, "But how could we do this?" "Let's make the collection basket a whole new reality," she said. "Have people pledge at the start of the school year how much they wish to contribute. Give it a big push, saying it could include stocks, bonds, wills, whatever. For those who wish, the monthly portion of their pledge could be taken out of their bank account just like a debit card. They could also make their donations over the Internet using our website. The technology to do this is simple and it fits current lifestyles. The collection basket would be for special causes and crisis situations. People could save up their small bills and loose change for the collection. Each week the money would be sent to some charitable cause chosen by the outreach committee. A box at the back of church would be for envelopes for those who still want to use them. Eventually the envelopes might be phased out as people get used to this new way of donating. What do you think of this? It is the way the rest of the world does business."

The stewardship committee and finance council looked stunned but it did make sense. Why not give it a try. The pastor gave his blessing and the new approach was inaugurated. This is where the management of politics came into play. People were reluctant to change their habits, especially when it involved their money and contributions. It took some doing, but slowly people caught on. It was easier for them because they didn't have to remember to bring their envelopes to church. "It's like an electronic plane ticket," one parishioner commented. "All I need to do is show up. Actually, I don't even need to do that anymore. Only I like putting my loose change in the collection basket. It feels as though I am helping out a worthy cause, as well as supporting the parish through my monthly pledge."

Polishing the Image

Ann Savage was pleased at what had taken place thus far. She was especially pleased that she and the pastor got along so well. Rather than just staying out of each other's way, they worked together on projects. The leaders and parishioners saw this and could see how well they complemented each other. Far from the leadership role of the pastor being diminished by the administrator, it was being enhanced. People came to see how wise he was to make this move and how comfortable he was in delegating his authority. This prepared the way for the next area of management Ann wanted to emphasize: managing the image. "Whether we like it or not," Ann told the staff at one of their meetings, "people will form an image or impression about us as a staff and about the parish as a whole. We might as well work at making it a good image." "How do we go about this?" the youth minister asked. "Easy," she replied. "You do it all the time with the teens. You try to find a 'cool' place to meet. You make up 'cool' T-shirts for the kids to wear. You print 'cool' posters and handouts about your events. You contact the 'cool' teens and try to get them to attend as a calling card for others. Once you do all this, does it really matter what the event is? You have created such a positive image that kids will think it is just the 'coolest thing going.' That is what I mean by managing the image. Let's see what we can do for the staff and the parish along this same line."

Starting with the staff, Ann tried to get them to picture the person in the back pew at the last Mass on Sunday. What image does that person have of the staff? "Unknown," "non-existent," "just the pastor," "not needed," "in-group" were some of the impressions that came to mind. "So how can we make the image more positive?" Ann asked. They brainstormed ideas, picked a few they liked and started to put them into operation. One was that the staff needed to be more visible to the parishioners. They decided to wear name tags at all parish events, to feature one staff person a month as an insert in the bulletin, to be the Eucharistic ministers at one of the Masses on the weekend, to be introduced as the parish staff to the congregation, to serve breakfast at the coffee and donuts following one of the morning Masses on Sunday. The one they liked the best was to have their feet washed on Holy Thursday and then go out to wash other people's feet in the congregation. It seemed to fit their perception of themselves as followers of Christ and servants to others.

This was one level of image building, but the more important one was the parish itself. Ann had worked hard when running the bank to establish its credibility through positive image building. The same could be done for the parish. What would make Holy Redeemer attractive to both parishioners and newcomers? What would make it visible in the surrounding area so that the larger community knew where it was and what it stood for? She called a combined meeting of the staff, council and leadership committees to see what they could suggest. During the course of the Saturday morning meeting, she divided the forty-five leaders into task groups. By the end of the morning each one was to have a plan for creating a more positive image at Holy Redeemer. One task group worked on young adults. If people in their twenties found the Church attractive, then anyone would. A second group worked on the ecumenical side of image, such as ways for building a positive relationship with other churches in the area. A third group was to work on the media, both written and electronic. A fourth was to enhance the environment around the church, making it inviting and attractive. The fifth task group was to work on first impressions, either as people came into church, called the parish on the phone or visited the parish's website.

Each of the five groups was to generate as many ideas as they could. They were then to choose one or two they liked best and start making plans to put them into practice. They could enlist others to help them get the job done, but a concrete plan with a specific time line had to be completed by noon. The creative energy in the room was infectious. As new ideas surfaced, group members clapped and shouted with delight. Suggestions were made that ranged from the sublime to the ridiculous. People vied with one another to come up with new and fresh ideas for improving the image of the parish. A large rendition of the mission statement hung on the wall as a guide and motivator for their work.

When time was called and the groups assembled to share their plans, their sense of pride and accomplishment were evident. The group working on young adults decided to concentrate on one Mass each weekend that would most appeal to this age group. They planned to go to the computer files and locate all the registered parishioners in this age group. They would send out an e-mail to the entire group, or at least to the ones that had an e-mail listed in the files. The young adults would be asked to be greeters, ushers, lectors, Eucharistic ministers, singers, gift bearers for at least one Mass a month. They would also be asked for ideas about how to make the parish more attractive to young adults. This, in itself, would start producing a positive image. It showed that the parish was interested in this group's input.

The second task group, the one working on image building with other churches, wanted to make sure the parish was not seen as being in competition with other faiths. To encourage greater cooperation, the group decided to sponsor a huge block party for all the churches. They would invite members from all the churches to attend, challenging each one to design a T-shirt from their congregation that could either be bought beforehand or at the block party. The task group would make the rounds of the churches, selling the idea and bringing sample T-shirts along to stir up interest. The churches could make their own T-shirts or have them done through Holy Redeemer for a discounted price. Prizes would be awarded at the block party for the best-designed T-shirt.

The group dealing with the media decided to concentrate on circulating fliers to the local motels and convention centers in town. The area where the parish was located had many visitors throughout the year who came for business and pleasure. Little had been done to let these people know about where the parish was located and the times of the Masses. The task group would get help designing the flier and then take it around to the motels for distribution in the rooms. They would also put an ad in the yellow pages and on cable television about the parish and what it had to offer.

The parish environment group was going to sponsor a "parish pride" weekend. Volunteers would help spruce up the grounds, plant more flowers and make the place "sparkle." The group was also going to design banners for the light posts on the street that would invite people into church and provide a colorful, upbeat tone along the road leading to the church.

The fifth group that was working on first impressions decided to create a more enticing and inviting phone message when people called the parish office. Rather than just getting a menu of possible options, the message would provide a more personal tone and include a "thought for the day." If the person they were calling was not available, then the message that people heard would have some spark and humor to it. "Showing people we care is the best message we could give," they said, "rather than having some boring message that suggests we are too busy to be bothered by their call."

What was reported was but a sampling of the many ideas generated during the morning. The leaders didn't want all this to be lost. They suggeste that a special committee on "image building" should be created to keep the momentum going. Ann and the pastor could not have been more pleased. "As you can see," Ann told the pastor, "just getting people to think something good is happening in the parish through positive image building does, in itself, create something good. People want it to happen and so it does."

Fostering a Covenant Parish

This story of Holy Redeemer and the contribution Ann Savage made as the administrator is but one example of what could be done to manage a modern Catholic parish. It is a complex task involving at least four different aspects. One is the management of structures and creating a plan for the future. Another is to uncover the potential of the parishioners themselves through volunteer recruitment and coordination. A third is to manage the inevitable conflicts and politics of the parish with strength and finesse. A fourth is managing the image which gives everyone a sense that something good is happening. This positive image is contagious, it gets people's attention and keeps them coming back.

Of course, good management is only one aspect of a parish. Of critical importance is good leadership, creative liturgies and taking the parish to the people. They all go hand in hand in creating a good parish. But a poorly managed parish in any one of the four aspects mentioned above is a messy place to attend and wears out both leaders and people. Eventually they grow weary and either go elsewhere or stop coming to church altogether. On the other hand, providing a well-managed parish in how it is structured, how people's energies and gifts are put to good use, how conflicts are faced and dealt with and how an attractive and positive image is maintained makes it a covenant parish which people want to join and become active members.

CHAPTER EIGHT

FORMING THE COVENANT:
GOING DEEPER

A parish is a definite community
of the Christian faithful,
established on a stable basis
within a particular church.

— CANON 515

In his book *The Parish in Catholic Tradition: History, Theology and Canon Law,* James Coriden expands on the above quotation from Canon Law to describe the parish as "a group of individuals and families who know each other, share common values and relate with one another." The *Dogmatic Constitution on the Church* from the Second Vatican Council describes parish this way:

> This Church of Christ is truly present in all legitimate local congregations of the faithful, which . . . are themselves called churches in the New Testament. For in their locality these are the new people called by God, in the Holy Spirit. . . . In turn the faithful are gathered together by the preaching of the gospel of Christ, and the mystery of the Lord's Supper is celebrated. . . . In these communities . . . Christ is present (*Lumen Gentium*, 26).

Throughout all ages, God has sought to enter into a mutual covenant of love with human beings. The Old Testament is filled with instances of Yahweh entering into close relationships with the Chosen People. The culmination and focal point of this covenant relationship is Jesus Christ, the embodiment of the union between God and ourselves.

To continue that covenantal relationship, Jesus found a way to maintain this intimate relationship with himself and with God. It was his covenant with us that is revealed in these words: "Unless you eat my flesh and drink my blood you shall not have life in you" (John 6:53). The locus of this intimate relationship is the local church, the parish. This is one place where the covenant of God with humankind is manifested. It is not the only place, of course, but it is a revelation of the covenant played out on many levels.

God's Friendship

Archbishop Rembert Weakland of the Milwaukee Archdiocese once gave a homily in which he asked the question, "Why come to Mass? Some people say, 'I can go out in the woods and commune with nature. This is where I find God. I don't need to come to church for that.' This is all quite true. But it is difficult to do this all by yourself. The Mass provides a help, a support, a direct connection with God, celebrated in the company of others who believe and pray with you to the same God."

The parish helps people connect with and enter into a personal relationship, a covenant, with their God. St. Ignatius Loyola, in the final week of the *Spiritual Exercises*, offers what he called "The Contemplation for Obtaining Love." The meditation begins by stating that love means giving yourself to the loved one in whatever way possible and that love is a mutual reality. Ignatius asked that the person consider all God has given and shared with the person, a complete self-disclosure. What, then, should be the person's response? Nothing less than a complete return of that love. "Take, Lord, receive, all that I have and possess," is the prayer Ignatius offers as an expression of this mutual love and friendship.

This is what a covenant relationship is all about: a complete and total gift of one's self. This is what lies at the heart of parish life, helping people discover and supporting them in their experience of God and of Jesus as Friend and Savior. A recent parish retreat for married couples and individuals was modeled on three aspects of spirituality: personal, relational and societal. The group had made an annual retreat together for many years and liked talking in small groups during the retreat weekend. In suggesting that part of the retreat be in silence so that people could spend time in quiet prayer, some resisted the idea. "We come to share community, not to be alone," they said. "People can pray on their own at some other time and place." Others thought it was worth trying. And so it happened. People were given questions and Scripture quotations to reflect on, as well as written materials to read if they got stuck. The questions were:

- How and when do I pray, either formally or informally?
- Where is God alive to me? Do I give God a chance to speak?
- Is life too hectic just now? Am I taking time for what matters?

The retreatants spent much of the morning in prayer. Some found it difficult but rewarding. "I never have the time for this," one woman remarked. "It is good to get back to the basics and just talk to God for a change."

This personal time with God is essential, and yet how difficult it is for people to find this time in their hectic lives. Parishes exist to help and challenge people to find the time to pray, to enter into a personal love relationship with God, to foster a covenant of friendship with the source of their being. The beginning of the second chapter of this book suggested one way to do this. Bishop Kenneth Untener's "Black Book" gave a quotation and a short reflection for each day during Lent, asking people to pray for six minutes on the reading. This is a simple, concrete way to help people discover God in their lives and to foster a friendship with God.

The staff and leaders of a parish must continually reflect on how to help people encounter God in their lives and to respond to the offer of God's friendship. They have to do this for themselves as well. What happens at Mass, for instance, that helps people pray? What readings or support materials are provided? What opportunities for learning how to pray exist in the parish? What occasions do people have to talk about their efforts and attempts at prayer?

Some parishes hand out a sheet as people leave church with the readings for the coming weekend, along with questions to reflect on over the week. Others make available after the Masses the *Living with Christ* booklet with the daily Scripture readings for the month (Novalis Publishers, Toronto, Canada, 800-387-7164). One pastor preached on different ways of praying during a month of homilies. Another parish provided spiritual direction for parishioners with a full-time paid staff person as a director.

She not only had people come to her directly, she also trained others to be mentors and directors in the parish.

"The parish is a definite community of the Christian *faithful* . . ." (Canon 515, emphasis added). One way to help people remain faithful is to help them discover God in their lives as Someone who wishes to enter into a love relationship, a personal covenant with them. The parish, however, is also a *community*. This is yet another aspect of covenant that needs to be explored.

Bonding with One Another

The communal side of covenant has many facets. One is the bond between family and friends. How can the parish foster these connections and help people remain true to their commitments? In a typical Catholic parish, most of the membership are married and have families of their own. A significant percentage, however, may be single and living alone. Most of these single people have close bonds with one or more persons in their lives. Some of those who are married, because of divorce or separation, may have families with children from more than one set of parents. Helping people sort out these complex relationships is a resource the parish could provide. Just acknowledging this complexity and realizing that many do not belong to a "typical" or traditional family can be supportive.

Inviting people to reflect and deepen their commitments to significant people in their lives can be helpful. The retreat referred to earlier did not only spend time on personal prayer but dealt with relational spirituality as well, helping people strengthen the bond with those they loved. The retreatants reflected on these questions:

- What is sacred in my loving and in my sexuality?
- Do I take the gift of intimacy for granted? Do I nourish it?
- What new "offsprings" are possible? What new ways can we be generative?

After some introductory remarks, people spent time first alone and then with their spouses or companions, sharing their insights. Finally, in groups of six to eight, they identified common issues and shared ideas with one another. They also reflected on the rituals they had established in their families or with the ones they loved which are the customs or traditions that manifest the love they have for each other. These rituals can also help them through the rough times and the periods of misunderstanding and conflict. The parish is well suited in helping people develop rituals in their personal lives. The liturgy and sacraments are filled with rituals that carry meaning that cannot be expressed in words. These practices and others like them need to be carried into one's personal life as well. Candles, flowers, cards, rings, mementos, poems, sayings, special apparel, dances, songs: These all communicate meaning and reflect the depth of the covenant and commitment people have with one another, a mutual bonding.

The parish does more than foster personal and relational covenants. It is *itself* a covenant and can be an expression of covenant in people's own lives. How is this manifested? First, among the leadership. In the dual-focus system of pastor and administrator suggested earlier, the two enter into a covenant with one another as co-leaders of the parish. The staff, too, should manifest a covenant relationship by making an agreement with one another to work in partnership as they direct the ministries of the parish.

Consider Immaculate Conception parish, a suburban church of 2500 families. It has a large staff and many active groups and ministries. The pastoral council was casting around for a theme for the coming year and hit upon, "The Parish as Covenant, A Joint Effort." They were not sure where it came from but it seemed to fit the emphasis they were looking for. They wanted a theme that would pull together all the various functions and aspects of the parish and bond them together. Up until now, parish groups operated on their own with few links or connections between them.

The council went to the staff and asked for ideas as to how to implement this theme for the coming year. The first reaction of the staff was, "How can *we* give the council any ideas? We need to get our own act together first. We don't operate as a covenant or a joint effort ourselves." It forced the staff, pastor and administrator included, to change its own way of interacting. They took a day away from the parish to see whether they could work more closely together. The result was a pledge they made to one another to operate as an interdependent body and not as individuals each working in separate areas. The covenant they drew up for themselves consisted of a set of ground rules that would govern their interaction. They pledged as a group:

1. To meet on a weekly basis for shared prayer, business and socializing
2. To speak freely and honestly with one another, sharing both positive and negative feelings
3. To listen openly and without pre-judging or making assumptions
4. To maintain confidences so that people felt safe in sharing ideas and insights in the group
5. To accept each person as an equal member of the group, pastor included
6. To support one another in their ministries and duties
7. To back one another up when confronted or criticized by others
8. To deal with staff conflicts directly, striving for an outcome in which all can be affirmed

Staff members returned home feeling a new and deeper bond between one another. They were confident that they could offer the council some ideas about how to proceed with the new theme and asked for a special meeting with the pastoral council to discuss options and possibilities. Only rarely had this happened in the past, emphasizing the need to change.

When the staff and council met together, the staff thanked the council for the challenge that the theme had been to the staff. They then shared what had happened at their own meeting, as well as the ground rules they had fashioned. The staff then asked that a covenant be formed between the staff and the council. "We need to be more of a joint effort ourselves," the pastor exclaimed. "I feel torn between the two groups. How can we work more collaboratively and in unison?" This surprised the council. They did not know the pastor and staff felt this way. They were eager, however, to work more closely with the staff. Many council members had felt intimidated by the staff and separated from them as a group. Dividing into pairs of one staff and one council member each, people exchanged ideas about how they might work more closely together. When they came together as a group, these were the ideas that surfaced. To start with, they needed more meetings like this one, at least twice a year, if not quarterly. There should be a staff representative besides the pastor as a full-fledged member of the pastoral council. Different staff members could make presentations to the council on a rotating basis so the council was more familiar with what they do. Both staff and council members could be commissioned together at the weekend Masses once a year. Also once a year, the staff and council could go away for a day together to discuss common issues and make joint plans for the parish. Most of all, these ideas should be affirmed in a covenant between staff and council. This covenant could be published in the bulletin, along with the new theme for the coming year. After some deliberation, this is the covenant agreed upon by the staff and council.

> We, the pastor, staff and pastoral council of Immaculate Conception parish, pledge to work together as partners for the good of the parish community, giving it leadership and spiritual direction. The staff provides professional resources to various areas of ministry. The pastoral council, in conjunction with the pastor, provides the overall direction, assessment and pastoral planning to the parish. Each body has a role and duty to perform but they do this in close interaction and mutual harmony with one another.

Once the staff and council had worked out their own convenantal issues and relationship, the next step was to deal with each area of parish ministry. One task of the pastoral council as a result of the new theme was to construct a Covenant Booklet for the leadership. Instead of a constitution and bylaws, the council decided to make up a new manual that would guide its own activities and those of all the other leadership bodies in the parish. The Covenant Booklet would include the mission statement of the parish and the statements of purpose for the council, staff and ministry groups of the parish. It would list all parish ministries and organizations and into which area they fit, whether worship, community, formation, outreach or administration. The booklet would include the covenant theme for the year and how this would be manifested by each aspect of parish life and operation. It would give a calendar of major events for the year, as well as the times and places for leadership meetings. It would include the process for arriving at decisions, including consensus and parish-wide discernment. Much of what would be contained in the Covenant Booklet would be developed throughout the year. Two obvious inclusions would be the staff's new ground rules and the joint pledge between staff and council. (See chapter four, p. 79, *A Yearly Tradition of Planning*, for more information about a Covenant Booklet.)

With a skeletal model of the Covenant Booklet in hand, council and staff members went to each area of parish ministry and asked them how they might exemplify in their work the new parish theme. How, for instance, would the area of worship and liturgy be a manifestation of the parish as covenant? The liturgy committee took this to heart and came up with these ideas: At the weekend Masses, especially when the Scripture reading of the Mass touched on God's covenant with the people, special rituals would be used to stress the bond the people have with God and with one another. Examples of covenant rituals would include renewal of marriage vows and baptismal promises, an emphasis on reconciliation and restoring God's graces through forgiveness, anointings with oil and songs related to covenant.

The community life committee discovered many ways for stressing covenant. Its very reason for existence was to foster a more welcoming, inclusive, accepting environment in the parish. The committee, pending an okay from the council, decided to hold a convention of the entire parish within six months. The theme would be "Forming Bonds Between Us." In preparation for this big event, all parish groups, organizations and ministries would be asked to hold their own mini-conventions. Their task would be to come up with one visible manifestation or symbol of how the parish is a joint effort. The convention itself would last two days, culminating with a dinner "under one tent." Everyone would be asked to bring a small, unfrosted cake that would be joined into one huge cake, frosted together and decorated with the words, "The Spirit of Immaculate Conception, Bonded Together as One Community." On the Saturday of the convention, each parish group would send representatives to a "House of Delegates." The task of this gathering would be to formulate a Covenant Document that would be ratified on Sunday at the parish-wide Mass. Saturday evening would be a time filled with skits and fun events for all ages. Sunday afternoon would be a single Mass of Unity, and in the evening a huge dinner would take place under the tent. The entire weekend would be a celebration of the "Parish As Covenant." It would have to be a joint effort of everyone if it was going to succeed. The committee realized this was a big undertaking, but given the right publicity and emphasis, along with good planning, it could be an event remembered for generations.

The education/formation committee, not to be outdone by community life, jumped at the idea of a parish convention. What a wonderful occasion for fostering small-group learning. The committee had tried to get this off the ground, but it needed a spark. This might be just what they were looking for. On the Sunday morning of the convention weekend, because there would be no parish Masses, only the Unity Mass in the afternoon, the committee decided to plan a "potpourri of potent topics." People would know ahead of time the topics to be discussed, ranging from "vanishing virginity" to "how much money is enough," from "Internet mania" to "drug heaven." Each topic would be discussed for thirty minutes in groups of five to ten plus a facilitator. People would have ten minutes of quiet time to sum up their thoughts. They would then move on to another topic with a new group for thirty minutes of sharing and ten minutes of reflection. That way, each person could be in two or three different groups during the morning. At the end of the morning, the entire group would assemble for reactions. They would then be invited to join a small group for the next six months to continue the dialogue. Groupings could be chosen according to a person's convenience, both the time of day and the day of the week. Between now and the convention, the committee would prepare the topics, line up and train facilitators and stir up interest in order to assure a large response.

For outreach, the committee working in this area decided to concentrate on raising awareness of the bond human beings have with Mother Earth. The Parish As Covenant was expanded to include "Our Covenant With the Blue Planet." Throughout the year, the outreach committee wanted to keep before the parishioners the fragile nature of the earth and the importance of keeping it healthy. The emphasis would be on discovering ways to consume less and recycle more, to tread lightly and waste not. The theme of the committee became, "Little Things Make All the Difference." First they made an inventory of how resources were used and reused in the parish. With this information in hand they made suggestions to parish groups on how to improve. For instance, at the coffee and donuts after Mass, people were invited to donate a mug. Volunteers made a large mug rack and hung it next to the coffee pots. Within a few weeks, no more styrofoam cups would be needed; reusable mugs would be used instead. Recycling bins were already located throughout the parish buildings. The outreach committee put up posters of the earth taken from a satellite to remind people how important reusing our resources was in saving the planet. Signs also appeared above light switches saying, "Let your light shine forth, but turn *this* one off when you leave." The outreach committee also published an article in the parish newsletter listing the results of their parish inventory and suggested new ways to conserve and recycle. It encouraged people to do the same in their homes and businesses, inviting people to submit new ideas and suggestions for what more could be done. "We have forgotten in this time of prosperity," one committee member wrote, "how limited our resources are. But raise the gasoline prices and our awareness returns. That only lasts as long as the problem exists. How quickly we return to using up our limited resources when the prices fall. Now is the time to think of using less rather than more. We are bonded with the earth, we are a large part of its survival. Treasure it as you do your family and loved ones. It feeds you and cares for you."

At first the people working on finance and administration did not have a clue as to how their area of ministry might exemplify "The Parish as Covenant." They put their heads together and came up with nothing. Then one member started to explore the word *covenant*, reflecting on Noah's ark and the rainbow God sent as a covenant with Noah after the flood. It was a pledge to never again destroy the world with a flood. "What is the pledge we in administration should make with the parish?" one member asked. "Perhaps it is a commitment to use the contributions people make in a way that benefits them and furthers God's reign." This started the group reflecting on how this might be done. Each year the administration and the finance committee makes a report to the parish. It is mostly just figures to show how income matched expenses and that the parish was on a solid financial footing, nothing very exciting or original.

"How about," one person suggested, "reporting it differently this year. Let's do a video for the end of the weekend Masses, followed by a discussion afterwards for those who wish. We will do it twice, once in December and again in June. The videos will be three to four minutes long. The first one will show what people's contributions have made possible in the parish and to those in the larger community. No more dollars and cents; make it creative and interesting. The theme could be, 'Look At What We Accomplished With Your Pledge.' We could go around to the ministries and activities and video what is going on. Get lots of shots of both old and young people smiling and enjoying themselves. At the second presentation in June we could show what we are planning to do in the coming year and how much revenue will be needed to be all we can be as a parish community. One person said, "Make the video short and to the point but still compelling." This captured the imaginations of the committee members. They immediately set about making plans for their "covenant videos."

In seeing all this activity and creativity, the pastoral council chairperson exclaimed at the next council meeting, "Look at all that our theme has produced. This has indeed become a joint effort."

Broader Implications

The local parish is not an independent entity. It is part of a diocesan structure, which itself is linked with the universal Church. The covenant a parish forms is not just with its own parishioners; it is in solidarity with the bishop, with other Catholic parishes and with the pope in Rome. Sometimes, as with any covenant, the interaction is life-giving and at other times it is a struggle. At the present moment, because of the shortage of priests, some aspects of parish life are being curtailed because there are not enough priests to preside at Eucharist, administer the sacraments or be spiritual leaders of the parish community. Many parishes have no resident clergy. The number of Masses is being cut back, services are not being offered. The situation will become much worse in the future if changes are not made in the requirements for priestly ordination. The covenantal relationship of the diocese with the Vatican, and the parish with the diocese, should be a mutual relationship, as between Yahweh and the Chosen People. Benefits accrue and demands are made by both parties. It is a joint effort at being Church. Parish communities, if they are to remain Catholic, will have to endure the struggles and losses that result from the shortages. They will also have to find a voice to make their concerns and issues known, similar to the insistence of the Syro-Phoenician woman pleading her case before Jesus. "Even the dogs under the table eat what the children leave" (Mark 7:28). She expanded Jesus' horizons about the scope of his ministry and what was possible. The local parish may have to do the same with the larger Church.

How this will play out in the future is not apparent. The hope is that it will be done with generosity and mutual respect, as is appropriate with any close bond or covenant between loving people. But consider the struggles of a parish where friction exists between leaders and people. St. Michael's is a multi-cultural parish with immigrants from Mexico, Puerto Rico, Central and South America, as well as long-standing members who have been a part of the parish for generations. The parish is now in flux. The pastor is close to retirement and finds the changes in clientele more than he can cope with. The longtime parishioners are resentful of the newcomers and are fearful of their own future in the area. The new people are themselves fearful of their status as Americans, many not having proper documentation. This parish is hardly a joint effort. The newly hired religious sister who is working with the immigrants has tried to discuss the situation with the pastor. His response is, "We have hired you to take care of the new people. You speak their language. Do what you can. The best that I can do is say Mass in Spanish and leave the preaching to the deacon." Sr. Janet is frustrated with this reaction. She is beginning to realize that if the parish is going to come together as a community, it will have to be up to her. The pastor is not well equipped for the task, nor does he have much motivation to do this.

Although Sr. Janet would prefer to speak directly to the pastor, she begins by approaching some of the older parishioners, especially those who have the ear and the confidence of the pastor. "Joe and Sam, you know the pastor. Help me out with how best to work with him effectively." This they do, initiating a weekly breakfast with the pastor and easing his fears. Eventually the men invite Sr. Janet to join them for breakfast and to talk over issues about the parish with the pastor. This becomes the first step toward direct interaction between the pastor and the pastoral associate. Up to this time he had left her to her own designs.

Sr. Janet also begins forming links within the Hispanic community. The people have come from many different cultures and traditions. Not only is it hard for them to be in an alien country; it is even difficult for them to understand one another even though they all speak the same language. She decides to form a Council of Hispanics as a place to air concerns and deal with fears. This takes time and patience because it is a foreign concept to them. The council begins by planning community events such as fiestas, potlucks and dances, as well as special ceremonies during the Spanish Mass. As the council members gain confidence in their tasks, she asks them to join the regular pastoral council for the monthly meetings. Part of the evening is spent in two groups, and part as a combination of the two functioning as one. Initially, the pastor remains with the English-speaking council and Sr. Janet with the Spanish-speaking group. When the two groups join together at the end, each shares with the other what they are planning and how they might work on projects together. The pastor likes this approach because it gives him a chance to exercise leadership while, at the same time, bringing in the Hispanic community. Without him realizing it, the pastoral associate is modeling a facilitating style of leadership with the Hispanic Council. She is empowering it to take on greater ownership as a leadership body among the Hispanic parishioners. The English-speaking council begins to notice this and tries to imitate this same way of acting at their own meetings. The pastor is pleased with this initiative. He is aware of new interest and energy among pastoral council members that had not been there before.

The combined councils begin to work on events that could bring the two communities together. One is a potluck of different ethnic foods one Sunday afternoon in October. This turns out to be a great success. People are proud of their dishes and enjoy trying out new and unique tastes from other countries. The parish Masses are the next step. The English and Hispanic choirs are combined for Christmas, singing carols from different lands and traditions. For Holy Week, the two groups come together to plan the services. This means that the pastor and the pastoral associate must work closely together in making sure the liturgies go smoothly in this bi-lingual environment. Slowly the parish begins to blend into a single covenant of believers. The pastor becomes more relaxed and open to this new direction. Sr. Janet, through patient endurance, is able to establish her position as co-leader of the entire community, not just of the Hispanics. She realizes that the pastor and herself still have much that is not in common. She has come to realize, however, that some things must be overlooked if the greater good is to be served. The pastor himself is growing more confident in his command of Spanish, even preaching on occasion. "It is never too late," he says to himself. "Maybe I will spend my vacation in Mexico this year and see what I can pick up to help my proficiency in Spanish."

The story of St. Michael's is a microcosm of what is possible in the Church as a whole. Sometimes the local parish and the diocesan or universal Church speak different languages. Rather than say it can never be resolved, seek to discover places of entry and areas of common interest. Look for individuals who are bridge-builders between groups and can act as liaisons. Find success in common projects and in planning joint events. Above all, pray. Our God is a God of covenant and relationships and expects the same of the Church.

Conclusion

It is at the local level that people encounter God, grow in faith and respond in service. The parish community is a critical ingredient in this development. Good leadership is at the core of a successful parish. What this book has attempted to do is offer an alternative to leadership that is dependent on just one person. The parish should be a joint effort of pastor and administrator, of staff and pastoral council, of coordinating groups in each area of parish ministry, of the People of God coming together for worship, community building, formation, service and outreach.

The parish is a covenant on many levels. Chapter one, for instance, focused on the covenant of partnership between pastor and one other person who together assume a joint share in the pastoring of the parish. The next chapter dealt with the complexity of pastoring. This includes both holding up the dream before the parish community, pointing to all that the parish could become as God's People, as well as calling people to move out of the routine and secure ways of operating and into a new way of being a covenant parish.

Chapter three centered on the effective use of time so that leaders and people alike did not become overwhelmed by their responsibilities. The alternative is to allow others to fill up what is lacking in one's own abilities and efforts in ministry. People are called to form a covenant within their own lives as a way of discovering what can be reasonably accomplished within the limited time and energy available.

The emphasis of chapter four was on looking ahead and discovering the full potential of the parish community. Creating a workable, efficient structure is of prime importance so there can be continuity and predictability in the parish. In this case, the parish covenant is spread out among many people and groups, all working together toward a common end.

Eucharist was the focus of chapter five. The task, as outlined in that chapter, is to form those who attend the parish liturgies into a covenant of believers, all united as a community in loving dialogue with their God. The responsibility of both the leaders of worship and the participants is to make the celebrations open and welcoming to all comers, to adapt and adjust the liturgies to fit diverse needs and inclinations, and to challenge the congregation to live out Eucharist in their daily lives. The covenant of worship, in other words, is a lifelong commitment, not one that is limited to that period when people participate in communal prayer and Eucharist.

The parish as covenant described in chapter six covered a wide spectrum that included active and inactive parishioners alike. The parish is people, not buildings or structures, rules or requirements. The manifestations of covenant included fostering closer bonds between parishioners through community-building events, as well as strengthening religious formation among people, especially by helping them cope with transitions in their lives. It also means challenging parishioners to open their hearts to those outside their own circle and to form bonds with those in need of support and assistance, and to connect with the alienated and inactive people by listening to their stories and learning from their experiences. The parish as covenant, in other words, has a wide scope and an inclusive definition.

Chapter seven returned to the practical side of parish as a call to pastoral partnership. The energies and experience of many people are needed in order to manage the parish well. Key leaders are essential in this effort. These are people who can manage the complexity of a parish, drawing in the timid and uninvolved, curtailing the dominant and opinionated, melding this diverse mixture of wants and desires, aspirations and insights into a unified effort.

The final chapter looked at the underlying purpose of parish as a help to its own members to grow in the knowledge and love of God, and as a force in the surrounding area of spiritual integrity, moral decision making and Christian service. Something new and wonderful is being fashioned on the local level of Church. As Yahweh said to Jeremiah:

> "Go down to the potter's house, and there I will let you hear my words." So I went down to the potter's house, and there he was working at his wheel. The vessel he was making of clay was spoiled in the potter's hand, and he reworked it into another vessel, as seemed good to him. Then the word of the Lord came to me: "Can I not do with you, O house of Israel, just as this potter has done?" says the Lord. "Just like the clay in the potter's hand, so are you in my hand, O house of Israel."
>
> —JEREMIAH 18:2–6

REFFERENCES:
A GUIDE TO FURTHER READING

Barna, George, Ed., *Leaders on Leadership: Wisdom, Advice and Encouragement on the Art of Leading God's People*, Ventura, CA: Regal Books, 1997.

The Canon Law Society, *The Code of Canon Law*, London: Collins Liturgical Publications, 1983.

Coles, Robert, *Lives of Moral Leadership*, New York: Random House, 2000.

Coriden, James, *The Parish in Catholic Tradition: History, Theology and Canon Law*, Mahwah, NJ: Paulist Press, 1997.

Covey, Steven, *Seven Habits of Highly Effective People*, New York: Simon and Schuster, 1989.

Cozzens, Donald B., *The Changing Face of the Priesthood*, Collegeville, MN: The Liturgical Press, 2000.

Dale, Robert D., *Leadership for a Changing Church: Charting the Shape of the River*, Nashville: Abingdon Press, 1998.

Forster, Patricia and Thomas P. Sweetser, SJ, *Transforming the Parish*, Franklin, WI: Sheed and Ward Publishers, 1994, 1999.

Friedman, Thomas L., *The Lexus and the Olive Tree*, New York: Farrar, Straus and Giroux, 2000.

Heifetz, Ronald, *Leadership without Easy Answers*, Cambridge, MA: Belknap Press of Harvard, 1994.

Markham, Donna J., *Spiritlinking Leadership: Working through Resistance to Organizational Change*, Mahwah, NJ: Paulist Press, 1999.

Muller, Wayne, *Sabbath, Restoring the Sacred Rhythm of Rest*, New York: Banton Books, 1999.

National Council of Catholic Bishops, *Our Hearts Were Burning Within Us*, Washington, D.C.: United States Catholic Conference Press, 1999.

Nuechterlein, Anne Marie and Celia Allison Hahn, *The Male-Female Church Staff: Celebrating the Gifts – Confronting the Challenges*, Washington, D.C.: The Alban Institute, 1990.

Parish Evaluation Project, *Parish Assessment and Renewal: A Process for Parish Strategic Planning*, 3195 S. Superior Street, Milwaukee, WI 53207, 414-483-7370, www.pepparish.org

Rolheiser, Ronald, *The Holy Longing, The Search for a Christian Spirituality*, New York: Doubleday, 1999.

Ryan, Ph.D., Penelope J., *Practicing Catholic: The Search for a Livable Catholicism*, New York: Henry Holt and Company, 1998.

Sims, Bennett, J., *Servanthood: Leadership for the Third Millennium*, Cambridge, MA: Cowley Publications, 1997.

Sweetser, SJ, Thomas P. and Mary Benet McKinney, OSB, *Changing Pastors*, Franklin, WI: Sheed and Ward Publishers, 1998.

Treat, James, Ed., *Native and Christian: Indigenous Voices on Religious Identity in the United States and Canada*, New York: Routledge, 1996.

Untener, Kenneth, *Preaching Better: Practical Suggestions for Homilists*, Mahwah, NJ: Paulist Press, 1999.

Wheatley, Margaret, *Leadership and the New Science: Learning About Organizations from an Orderly Universe*, San Francisco: Barrett-Koehler Publishers, Inc., 1992.

Wilkes, Paul, *Excellent Catholic Parishes, A Guide to Best Places and Practices*, Mahwah, NJ: Paulist Press, 2001.

_____, *The Good Enough Catholic, A Guide for the Perplexed*, New York: Ballantine Books, 1996.

INDEX